Florida Seashore & Wildlife

Written and Illustrated
by Todd Telander

T0346357

FALCONGUIDES ®

GUILFORD, CONNECTICUT
HELENA, MONTANA

AN IMPRINT OF GLOBE PEQUOT PRESS

MIX
Paper from
responsible sources
FSC® C005010

Copyright © 2014 Morris Book Publishing, LLC
Illustrations copyright © 2014 Todd Telander

FalconGuides is an imprint of Globe Pequot Press.
Falcon, FalconGuides, and Outfit Your Mind are registered trademarks of Morris
Book Publishing, LLC.

Illustrations: Todd Telander
Project Editor: Staci Zacharski
Text Design: Sheryl P. Kober
Layout Artist: Sue Murray

Library of Congress Cataloging-in-Publication Data
Telander, Todd, author, illustrator.
  Falcon pocket guide : Florida seashore & wildlife / written and illustrated by
Todd Telander. — First [edition].
     pages cm. — (Falcon pocket guides)
  Summary: "Falcon Pocket Guides are full-color, visually appealing, on-the-go
guides for identifying plants and animals and learning about nature. "— Pro-
vided by publisher.
  Summary: "Falcon Pocket Guide: Florida Seashore & Wildlife is a field guide to
180 of the most commonly found shells, plants, and animals along Florida's coast.
Anatomically correct illustrations and detailed descriptions make it easy to iden-
tify flora and fauna throughout Florida's coastline. Informative and beautiful to
peruse, this is the essential resource when you're out in the field. Falcon Pocket
Guides are full-color, visually appealing, on-the-go guides for identifying plants
and animals and learning about nature"— Provided by publisher.
  ISBN 978-0-7627-8187-4 (pbk.)
  1. Seashore animals—Florida—Identification. I. Title. II. Title: Florida seashore
& wildlife.
  QH105.F6T45 2014
  591.769'9—dc23

                                                          2013029035

Printed in the United States of America

10 9 8 7 6 5 4 3 2 1

To my wife, Kirsten, my children, Miles and Oliver, and my parents,
all of whom have supported and encouraged me through the years.

Contents

Introduction

Welcome to the Sunshine State! Home to an abundance of fascinating wildlife, Florida combines the temperate influence of mainland North America with the tropical influence of the Gulf of Mexico and the Atlantic Ocean. Although the elevation never reaches more than 350 feet, Florida encompasses a wide array of habitats, from dry prairies and pine sandhill forests to swamps, marshes, beaches, mangroves, and an extensive coastline with coral reefs. Living in this varied region are multitudes of mammals, birds, reptiles, amphibians, fish, butterflies, and other invertebrates, including some species found nowhere else in the continental United States, such as the American crocodile and the diminutive Key deer. This guide is meant to be an overview of the vast diversity of wildlife in Florida, an introduction to some of the most common and distinct species that call this land home, and a starting point for your explorations of this unique state.

Notes about the Species Accounts

Names

Both the common name and the scientific name are included for each entry. Since common names tend to vary regionally, and there may be more than one common name for each species, the universally accepted scientific name of genus and species (such as *Mimus polyglottos* for the northern mockingbird) is more reliable to be certain of identification. Also, you can often learn interesting facts about an animal by understanding the English translation of its Latin name. For instance, the generic name, *Mimus,* means "a mimic," and *polyglottos* means "many voices," alluding to the varied songs that the mockingbird copies.

Size

Most measurements of size refer to overall length, height, or weight. For animals with long tails, antennae, or other appendages, those measurements may be given separately from those of the body. Butterfly and moth measurements refer to wingspan. Size may vary considerably within a species (due to age, sex, or environmental conditions), so use a measurement as a general guide, not a rule.

Range

Range refers to the geographical area where a species is likely to be found, such as the Keys, the Panhandle, central Florida, the Gulf Coast, etc. Some species may be found throughout their range, whereas others prefer very specific habitats within their range. Also mentioned under this heading is the season during which the species is present in Florida. For migratory birds, and for some butterflies, the season is the time when the greatest number of individuals occurs in Florida. Some species are year-round residents, some may spend only summers or winters here, and some may be transient, only stopping during the spring or fall migrations. Even if only part of the year is indicated for a species, be aware that there may be individuals that arrive earlier or remain for longer than the given timeframe. Most land-dwelling animals are year-round residents. Some fish may arrive in seasonal migrations.

Habitat

An animal's habitat is one of the first clues to its identification. Note the environment (including vegetation, climate, elevation, substrate, presence or absence of water) where you see an animal and compare it with the description listed. Some common habitats in Florida include coral reefs, coastal dunes, salt marshes, mangroves, cypress swamps, hammocks, pine sandhills, river and spring systems, urban areas, scrublands, and prairies.

Illustrations

The illustrations show adult animals in the coloration they are most likely have in Florida. Many species show variation in different geographical areas, in different seasons, or between the sexes. Birds show this variety most often, so I have illustrated males and females when they look different. Other variations, such as seasonal color changes in some mammals and variable patterns in fish, are described in the text.

Useful Scientific Terms

I have, for the most part, used familiar language to describe the animals in this book, but their are occasions when it makes more sense to use some terms developed by the scientific community, especially when referring to body parts. In particular, terms associated with birds, fish, and butterflies are described below:

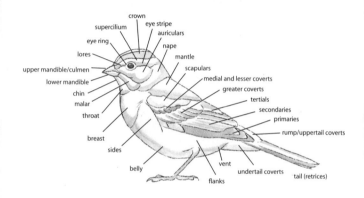

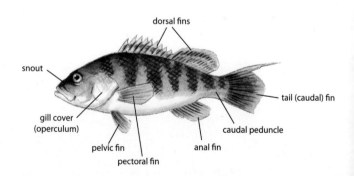

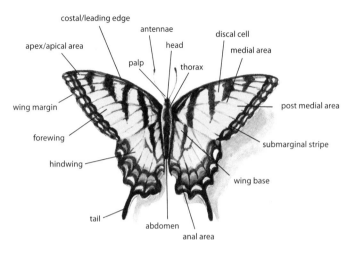

costal/leading edge

antennae

head

apex/apical area

palp

thorax

discal cell

medial area

wing margin

post medial area

forewing

submarginal stripe

hindwing

wing base

tail

abdomen

anal area

MAMMALS

Nine-banded Armadillo, *Dasypus novemcinctus*
Family Dasypodidae (Armadillos)
Size: 31" including tail
Range: Throughout Florida except for the Keys
Habitat: Woodlands, scrub, areas with sandy or moist soils

The nine-banded armadillo is a curious, largely tropical mammal with an armored back made of small plates of hornlike material. It has a pointed head, large ears, short limbs, a long, scaled tail that is about the same length as the body, and stout claws for digging. Its color is uniformly gray. Armadillos are mostly solitary, and are active during hours of low light, when they forage on the ground for insects, worms, fruit, eggs, and other invertebrates, lapping up food with their sticky tongues. They are excellent diggers, make extensive burrow systems, and are comfortable in the water.

Virginia Opossum, *Didelphis virginiana*
Family Didelphidae (Opossums)
Size: 30" with tail
Range: Throughout Florida
Habitat: Woodlands, riparian zones, urban areas with trees, farms

The Virginia opossum is a marsupial, meaning it bears premature young that develop in an external pouch, and is the only member of this group in North America. It is stocky, with relatively small limbs, a pointed snout, and a long, round, hairless tail. Its color is mottled grayish with a white face and dark ears. It is nocturnal, mostly solitary, and reasonably adept at swimming and climbing. It has a highly varied diet that includes nuts, fruit, insects, small animals, and carrion. Opossums have a curious habit of feigning death when under attack, then resuming as normal once safe.

3

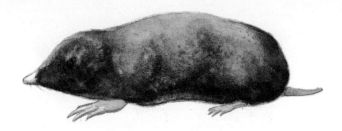

Eastern Mole, *Scalopus aquaticus*
Family Talpidae (True Moles)
Size: 6" with tail
Range: Throughout Florida
Habitat: A variety, including fields, woodlands, lawns, areas with dry,
loose soils

Also known as the common mole, the eastern mole is a small,
stocky, sturdy mammal with a body shape well designed for life
underground. The body is elongate and tube-shaped, with narrow hips, a pointed, fleshy snout, and a short tail for navigating
though tunnels, which it digs with its broad, spadelike forelimbs
and long, thick claws. The coat is short, velvety, deep gray-brown
above and slightly paler below. The eyes are tiny and covered
by skin, and the ears are invisible beneath the fur. Eastern moles
build tunnels within which they forage for earthworms, insects,
and some plants. They are responsible for creating conspicuous
dirt mounds at the entrance to their tunnels.

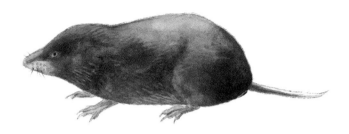

Southern Short-tailed Shrew, *Blarina carolinensis*
Family Soricidae (Shrews)
Size: 3–5" with tail
Range: Throughout Florida
Habitat: Moist woodlands, brushy areas

Shrews are the smallest mammals in North America, and are unrelated to rodents. The southern short-tailed shrew is very active. It is shaped like an elongate mouse with a sharply pointed head, tiny eyes, no external ears, and a short, lightly furred tail. The fur is dense, dark gray above, and slightly paler below. This shrew is active both day and night, mostly solitary, and digs an extensive network of tunnels. Voracious feeders, these shrews forage within their tunnels and nearby leaf litter for insects, earthworms, spiders, small invertebrates, and sometimes nuts and seeds. They can also secrete poisonous saliva that paralyzes their prey.

Big Brown Bat, *Eptesicus fuscus*
Family Vespertilionidae (Vespertilionid Bats)
Size: 5" with tail
Range: Central and northern Florida
Habitat: A wide variety including woodlands, buildings, and caves

As a group, bats are the only mammals that truly fly, using wings made of a thin membrane stretched across elongated forearms and fingers. The big brown bat is a widely distributed, fairly large bat with fur that is brown above and lighter below, with blackish wing membranes. There is a fleshy projection at the base of the ear (the tragus), which is short and rounded. Big brown bats are nocturnal, roosting by day in dark, secluded areas such as caves or old buildings. They emerge at night to forage for beetles and other insects, locating them primarily by echolocation, emitting high-pitched chirps and receiving reflected sound with their complex, large ears.

Brazilian Free-tailed Bat, *Tadarida brasiliensis*
Family Molossidae (Free-tailed Bats)
Size: ~4" with tail
Range: Throughout Florida
Habitat: Caves, buildings, and surrounding environs

Also known as the Mexican free-tailed bat or guano bat, the Brazilian free-tailed bat is a small bat with narrow wings and a tail that projects freely about halfway past the interfemoral membrane, a patch of skin that stretches between the legs. The fur is rich brown, slightly darker above than below, and the wings are blackish. The ears are broad, reaching forward on the face, and the upper snout is wrinkled. Brazilian free-tailed bats emerge from roosting sites at night in large groups and forage in the air for a variety of insects, using echolocation to zero in on prey. These bats are among the most numerous mammals in the United States, famous for gathering in enormous concentrations in caves in New Mexico and for the deep deposits of guano accumulated in those caves.

7

Florida Mouse, *Podomys floridanus*
Family Muridae (Mice and Rats)
Size: 7.5" with tail
Range: Central and northern Florida
Habitat: Dry, sandy areas with oak and palmetto scrub

Also known as the gopher mouse or big-eared mouse, the Florida mouse is relatively large with big ears and eyes, elongated hind feet, and a thin, medium-length furred tail. It is orange-brown above, darkest on the back, and whitish below and on the bottom half of the head. It is primarily nocturnal, feeds on seeds, insects, and invertebrates, and utilizes the existing burrows of gopher tortoises or other rodents. Florida mice are found only in Florida.

Florida Wood Rat, *Neotoma floridana*
Family Muridae (Mice and Rats)
Size: 21" with tail
Range: Central and northern Florida; also Key Largo
Habitat: Woodlands, hedgerows, palmetto scrub

The Florida wood rat was once considered the eastern wood rat, along with the Allegheny wood rat (with a more northerly range), but now these are considered distinct species. The Florida wood rat is a chunky, large rodent with a squarish head, large ears, and hairy tail that is usually slightly less long than the rat's body length. The fur is grayish-brown above and white below and on the feet. Florida wood rats are nocturnal, breed year round, and feed on plant matter and seeds, as well as fungi. They build houselike nests of sticks and debris in crevices, burrows, or caves, which offer them protection and a place to cache food. They are members of the "pack rat" group, known to collect bits of small metallic refuse.

Eastern Fox Squirrel, *Sciurus niger*
Family Sciuridae (Squirrels)
Size: 24–30" with tail
Range: Throughout Florida
Habitat: Open, mature woodlands of pine, oak, mangrove, cypress

The eastern fox squirrel is a large tree squirrel (much larger than the eastern gray squirrel) with a long, bushy tail. It occurs in variable color morphs: The body can be anywhere from rusty brown to grayish to all black above, with the underside whitish or tawny. A common darker form found in Florida is gray-brown with a black face and a white muzzle and chin. Eastern fox squirrels are generally solitary as they search in trees or on the ground for nuts, buds, and berries. In the fall, nuts are cached in tree cavities or large nests that they construct from leaves in the crotches of trees.

Eastern Gray Squirrel, *Sciurus carolinensis*
Family Sciuridae (Squirrels)
Size: 18" with tail
Range: Throughout Florida
Habitat: Mixed hardwood forests, parks, suburbs

The widespread and common eastern gray squirrel is a social, arboreal, relatively large squirrel with a long, very bushy tail and large eyes. Its color is gray, sometimes with a brownish cast, and whitish below, with pale eye rings. The tail is edged with white-tipped hairs. Active most times of the day, these squirrels forage for nuts, fruits, seeds, insects, eggs, and fungi, and may store nuts in ground caches. They use tree cavities to nest in, or may build large nests of twigs and leaves high in a tree.

Southern Flying Squirrel, *Glaucomys volans*
Family Sciuridae (Squirrels)
Size: 9" with tail
Range: Throughout Florida except for the Keys
Habitat: Coniferous or deciduous woodlands, oak hammocks

The southern flying squirrel is a small, unusual squirrel designed to glide (not fly) from tree to tree or from tree to ground. Flaps of skin connect the front and rear feet: When outstretched, these flaps allow the squirrel to glide more than 100 feet and make a delicate landing. The color is grayish brown, darker along the flanks, and whitish below. These squirrels are active at night and are highly social, with several individuals sometimes sharing a nest site in a tree cavity or external structure. They forage for nuts, fruit, insects, fungus, and eggs, and store food in tree cavities for winter use.

Nutria (Coypu), *Myocastor coypus*
Family Myocastoridae (Nutrias)
Size: 24" body; 15" tail
Range: Throughout Florida except for the Keys
Habitat: Swamps, lakesides

The nutria is a large rodent native to South America that was originally brought to the United States as a source of commercial fur. It is now naturalized in lowland, marshy areas of Florida. It has a sausage-shaped body with small ears, a long, round, hairless tail, and webbed rear feet. Its fur is yellowish or brownish gray and is composed of a dense, soft undercoat covered by shaggier top hairs. Quite social, nutrias are mostly nocturnal and make burrows in the banks at the water's edge. They are excellent swimmers, and they forage for aquatic plants or small aquatic animals.

American Beaver, *Castor canadensis*
Family Castoridae (Beavers)
Size: 28" body; 10" tail
Range: Throughout Florida, primarily in the northern regions
Habitat: Ponds, lakes, streams with adjacent woodlands

Once nearly extirpated because of hunting and trapping for pelts, this largest of North American rodents now covers most of its original range. The beaver is heavy and compact, with webbed rear feet, large front incisors, and a long, dexterous, scaled, flattened tail. The color is dark brown. Beavers are known for cooperative construction of impressive dams and lodges made from trees they have felled. Their presence is often announced by a loud tail slap on the water. Mostly nocturnal, they eat the tender, inner bark of trees, as well as small branches and buds.

Eastern Cottontail Rabbit, *Sylvilagus floridanus*
Family Leporidae (Rabbits and Hares)
Size: 14"
Range: Throughout Florida except for the Keys
Habitat: Drier areas of brush, thickets, upland fields

The eastern cottontail is a relatively small rabbit, colored gray brown to reddish brown, with a short, rounded, white tail (hence the common name), and long ears. The eyes are quite large, and the rear feet are long and powerful. The cottontails' high rate of reproduction and general abundance make them an important food source for carnivorous wildlife. Eastern cottontails are mostly nocturnal, but can be seen feeding at almost any time on grasses, herbs, branches, and bark. The rabbits never stray too far from brushy cover or their burrows.

Marsh Rabbit, *Sylvilagus palustris*
Family Leporidae (Rabbits and Hares)
Size: 17"
Range: Throughout Florida
Habitat: Most wetland environments, including swamps, lakesides, coastal lowlands

The marsh rabbit is a smaller version of the eastern cottontail with a preference for marshy habitats—either freshwater or salt water. The fur is coarse; the color is brownish-gray above, lighter on the belly, and is reddish brown on the nape and feet. The ears are relatively small and the tail is grayish brown, unlike the white of the cottontail. Marsh rabbits forage on all manner of wetland vegetation, including twigs, grasses, bulbs, tubers, and leaves. As a defense, they will run to water and partially submerge, leaving only the upper part of their heads above water. They also have a curious habit of walking erect on their hind legs.

Raccoon, *Procyon lotor*
Family Procyonidae (Ringtails and Raccoons)
Size: 34" with tail
Range: Throughout Florida
Habitat: Woodlands, streams or lakesides, urban areas

The raccoon is a highly adaptable mammal, equally at home in remote forests or urban centers. It is stocky and heavy, with a short, masked face and a bushy coat. Its color is pale gray mixed with black, with a tail ringed in black and gray. Incredibly dexterous fingers allow it to undo knots and even work doorknobs. Raccoons are primarily nocturnal and may be seen alone or in small groups. They prefer to feed near a water source, often dipping their food in water first, and will eat just about anything, including fruits, nuts, insects, fish, crayfish, and worms.

Striped Skunk, *Mephitis mephitis*
Family Mephitidae (Skunks)
Size: 22" with tail
Range: Throughout Florida
Habitat: Woodlands, brush, suburban parks; usually near a water source

The striped skunk is known primarily for its ability to elude danger by spraying a noxious fluid from an anal duct. It is a stocky, weasel-like mammal with a long, bushy tail and long front claws for digging. Its color is black with broad white stripes running down its sides, merging into a white stripe on the upper part of the tail. Usually solitary, striped skunks stay in dens during the day and forage at night. Being omnivorous, they eat a wide variety of foods including fruit, nuts, insects, small mammals, and eggs.

Eastern Spotted Skunk, *Spilogale putorius*
Family Mephitidae (Skunks)
Size: 18" with tail
Range: Throughout Florida except the Keys
Habitat: Brushy open woodlands, coastal scrub, grasslands; usually near a water source

The eastern spotted skunk is smaller than the striped skunk but shares its defensive ability to spray a noxious liquid from ducts near its anus. It is weasel-like, with fine, soft fur, a thick, bushy tail, and long claws. Its color is black, with variable and irregular white spotting and striping on the head and back and a white-tipped tail. Solitary and nocturnal, these skunks stay in dens during the day. They can climb trees but mostly forage on the ground, eating a variety of foods including fruit, insects, small mammals, birds, and eggs.

American Mink, *Mustela vison*
Family Mustelidae (Weasels and Otters)
Size: 20" with tail
Range: Central and northern Florida
Habitat: Coastal areas, streams, marshes

The American mink is an elongate, short-legged member of the weasel family with a long tail, webbed feet, and a semiaquatic lifestyle. Its luxurious pelt is dark blackish brown; minks sometimes have a whitish area around the mouth and may have pale spotting on their undersides. Minks are mostly nocturnal and solitary, are excellent swimmers, and never stray too far from a water source. They are carnivores, eating aquatic animals and invertebrates, but will also take birds, eggs, and rabbits. A subspecies of mink known as the Everglades mink resides in marshes in the Everglades and feeds mostly on aquatic prey.

River Otter, *Lontra canadensis*
Family Mustelidae (Weasels and Otters)
Size: 4' with tail
Range: Throughout Florida except for the Keys
Habitat: Areas near streams, lakes, or estuaries

The river otter is a large, curious, and playful member of the weasel family with a mostly aquatic lifestyle. It is elongate and sinuous, with small ears, webbed feet, and a long, somewhat thickened tail to aid in swimming. Its fur is thick, dark brown above and pale gray below and across the lower face. River otters are social and often travel in small family groups. They hunt primarily in the water for fish, amphibians, or aquatic invertebrates. They live in burrows near water and form well-used trails along the shore or between water sources.

Long-tailed Weasel, *Mustela frenata*
Family Mustelidae (Weasels and Otters)
Size: 14" with tail
Range: Throughout most of Florida
Habitat: Woodlands, fields with brushy cover, often near water

The long-tailed weasel is a wily, small, elongate, long-necked predator, and one Florida's smallest meat eaters. It is reddish brown with buff underparts and throat and a black tip on its long tail. It is nocturnal and solitary, an excellent climber, and, due to its thin, sinuous shape and short legs, it can slip into burrows to attack rodents living within. Long-tailed weasels also hunt rabbits, birds, eggs, and fish. To den, they use the existing burrows of other, similar-size rodents.

Florida Panther (Puma), *Puma concolor*
Family Felidae (Cats)
Size: 7' body; 2.5' tail (males larger than females)
Range: South-central and southwest Florida
Habitat: Open to dense woodlands, brush, swamps, hammocks

The Florida panther (also known as the puma, mountain lion, or cougar) is a huge (about 125 pounds), reclusive, powerful cat that is currently endangered. The cat is the official state animal. It has a long tail, and its fur is a blend of tawny browns, tans, and grays, paler on the underside and white on the chest and throat. The tail tip is dark brown, as are the backs of the ears and marks on the muzzle. Florida panthers are mostly solitary except during breeding season or when with kittens. They hunt by stealth, waiting on rocky ledges or trees for prey to pass, or slink through grass to ambush their prey, which includes deer, elk, and smaller mammals.

Bobcat, *Lynx rufus*
Family Felidae (Cats)
Size: 28" body; 5" tail
Range: Throughout Florida except in the Keys
Habitat: A wide variety of habitats, including forests, riparian areas, scrub

The bobcat is about double the size of a housecat, is well cam-ouflaged, and has a very short, "bobbed" tail. Its face appears wide due to long fur tufts below the ears, and the ears are tipped with short, black hairs. The color is light brown to reddish above, pale or whitish below, and spotted with dark brown or black that sometimes is streaked on the animal's legs. The tail is striped, and black along the top edge. Bobcats are typically active during early morning hours and after dusk, except in winter when they are active during the day. They hunt by stealth, ambushing their favored prey of rabbits, other small mammals, and birds.

Coyote, *Canis latrans*
Family Canidae (Coyotes and Foxes)
Size: 4' with tail
Range: Throughout Florida except for the Keys
Habitat: Open country, scrub, grasslands

The coyote is an intelligent and adaptable canid that has been able to survive in a wide variety of habitats and in spite of persecution by humans. It looks like an average-size dog, with a long, thin muzzle and pointed ears. The color can range from gray to light brown or reddish. It has a bushy tail that is held low or between the legs. Coyotes hunt alone or in small packs, primarily during the night. Their diet is varied, and they scavenge for anything edible, including rodents, rabbits, snakes, berries, insects, and carrion.

Gray Fox, *Urocyon cinereoargenteus*
Family Canidae (Coyotes and Foxes)
Size: 3' with tail
Range: Throughout Florida except for the Keys
Habitat: Open woodlands, hammocks, suburban areas

The gray fox is a small, stealthy, nimble canid with a bushy tail and
the ability to climb trees using its short, curved, retractable claws.
Its fur is gray and white-speckled above, reddish along the sides
and legs, and there is a black streak down the back and tail, end-
ing in a black tail tip. The muzzle is thin and small, while the ears
are comparatively large. They are mostly solitary and nocturnal,
and feed on a varied diet including rabbits, rodents, insects, nuts,
and fruit.

Red Fox, *Vulpes vulpes*
Family Canidae (Coyotes and Foxes)
Size: 38" with tail
Range: Northern Florida and in the Panhandle
Habitat: Open woodlands, fields, brushy areas; may approach urban centers

Like other foxes, the red fox is a wily, secretive, adaptable, doglike mammal with a small muzzle, large ears, and a bushy tail. It is rusty red above, white or gray below, with black "stockings" on the legs and a white-tipped tail. Color variations may include black, slate gray, or a dark cross along the shoulders. Red foxes are solitary hunters and are most active at night or in the twilight hours, seeking the shelter of a den during the day. They feed on small mammals, insects, carrion, plants, and berries, sometimes performing a dramatic leaping pounce to catch rodents.

American Black Bear, *Ursus americanus*
Family Ursidae (Bears)
Size: 3' tall at the shoulder; 6' tall standing (males larger than females)
Range: Throughout Florida expect in the Keys
Habitat: Forests, wooded swamps, open range

Although the smallest bear in North America, the American black bear is still a heavy (up to 600 pounds), lumbering bear with thick (but not humped) shoulders, short legs, and small ears and tail. There is variation across its range, but in Florida its color is black, with a light brown muzzle and sometimes a white patch on the chest. Black bears feed mostly at night, covering large areas of land while foraging for plants, roots, berries, grubs, and occasionally small animals, fish, and carrion. The black bear is usually solitary, except in mating season or in family units of cubs and a mother. The bear spends most of the winter hibernating in a den, but can be aroused quickly.

Wild Boar (Feral Pig), *Sus scrofa*
Family Suidae (Wild Boars, Hogs, Pigs)
Size: 4' body; 6" tail
Range: Throughout Florida except in the Keys
Habitat: Forests, open woodlands, swamps

Wild boars are either feral populations of domesticated pigs, intro-duced wild boars from Europe, or hybrids of the two. They have stocky bodies with short, thin legs and large heads with protrud-ing snouts. They can achieve weights of up to 200 pounds, and the male wild boar has canines that are enlarged into tusks. The hair is bristly and thick and varies in color from black to brownish to white. Quick and quite aggressive, wild boars are active mostly during the morning and evening, and can be found alone or in groups. They forage on the move, digging up roots and tubers, grazing on plants, and hunting insects.

White-tailed Deer, *Odocoileus virginianus*
Family Cervidae (Deer)
Size: 6' body; 10" tail
Range: Throughout Florida
Habitat: Dense forest, forest edges, swamps

North America's smallest deer, the white-tailed deer is a secretive mammal of thick forests. It is very agile, fast, and able to outmaneuver most predators. The male has antlers with a main beam that supports smaller prongs. The color of its fur is reddish brown with a white belly and throat. When alarmed, the white-tailed deer raises its tail, revealing the brilliant white underside, hence its colloquial name of "flagtail." White-tailed deer travel in small groups in summer, but in winter may congregate in larger herds. Being herbivores, they forage for grasses, herbs, and nuts. A much smaller version of this species, known as the Key deer, is endangered and found only in the Florida Keys.

West Indian Manatee, *Trichechus manatus*
Family Trichechidae (Sea Cows)
Size: 8–12'
Range: Throughout coastal Florida and in major rivers
Habitat: Coastal bays and estuaries; inland rivers and springs

The West Indian manatee, commonly known as the manatee, is a large, plump, aquatic mammal with a cylindrical body that is tapered at both ends. Strangely, it is able to move freely between salt- and freshwater environments. It has two clublike forelimbs with nails, no dorsal fin, and a horizontally flattened tail shaped like a large paddle. The head has a broad, whiskered muzzle and tiny eyes. The skin is thick and tough, colored in variable shades of gray, and often supports growths of algae and barnacles. Usually quite slow moving, manatees lazily forage for aquatic plants and grasses. They are mostly solitary, but may congregate during the winter in warm, inland springs.

Bottlenose Dolphin, *Tursiops truncatus*
Family Delphinidae (Ocean Dolphins)
Size: 8–12' (males larger than females)
Range: Throughout coastal Florida and in major rivers
Habitat: Coastal waters, bays, estuaries, mouths of major rivers

The bottlenose dolphin is widespread in Florida's waters and across the globe in tropical oceans. Agile and playful, it travels in groups known as pods (sometimes containing more than one hundred individuals), and is the dolphin most often seen at aquatic shows or riding the wakes of ships. It is a sleek, flexible, marine mammal with a bottle-shaped snout, a triangular dorsal fin, and a blowhole for breathing at the top of its head. The skin is smooth, dark gray above, medium gray along the sides, whitish on the belly and throat, with some darker streaking forward and behind the eyes. Bottlenose dolphins prey mostly on fish and squid, which they hunt with the help of echolocation, chasing them down by swimming quickly.

BIRDS:
NONPASSERINES

Wood Duck, *Aix sponsa*
Family Anatidae (Ducks and Geese)
Size: 18"
Range: Throughout Florida; year-round
Habitat: Wooded ponds and swamps

The regal wood duck is a dabbling duck, which tip head first into shallow water to pluck aquatic plants and animals from the bottom. The male is long-tailed and small-billed, with a dark back, light buff-colored flanks, and sharp black-and-white head patterning. The male also sports a bushy head crest that droops behind the nape. The female is gray-brown with spotting along the underside and a conspicuous white, teardrop-shaped eye patch. Both sexes swim with their heads angled downward as if in a nod, and they have sharp claws used to cling to branches and snags. The illustration shows a breeding male, below, and a female, above.

Mallard, *Anas platyrhynchos*
Family Anatidae (Ducks and Geese)
Size: 23"
Range: Northern and central Florida; year-round
Habitat: Virtually any water environment, including those in parks and urban areas

The ubiquitous mallard is the most abundant duck in the Northern Hemisphere. It is a classic dabbling duck, plunging its head underwater with its tail up as it searches for aquatic plants, animals, and snails, although it will also eat worms, seeds, insects, and even mice. Noisy and quacking, it is a heavy but strong flier. The male has a dark head with green or blue iridescence, a white neck ring, and a large yellow bill. His underparts are pale, with a chestnut-brown breast. The female is plain brownish with buff-colored, scalloped markings. She also has a dark eye line and an orangey bill with a dark center. The speculum is blue on both sexes, and the tail coverts often curl upward. Mallards form huge floating flocks called "rafts." To achieve flight, a mallard lifts straight into the air without running. The illustration shows a breeding male, below, and a female, above.

Bufflehead, *Bucephala albeola*
Family Anatidae (Ducks and Geese)
Size: 14"
Range: Northern and central Florida; winter
Habitat: Inland lakes and sheltered coastal bays

The bufflehead is a diminutive diving duck—indeed, the small-est duck in North America. Also known as the bumblebee duck, it forms small flocks as it forages open water for aquatic plants and invertebrates. The puffy, rounded head seems large for the body and the small, gray-blue bill. The breeding male is striking, with a large white patch on the back half of his head, contrast-ing with the black front of his head and back. His underside is white. The female is paler overall, with a dark, gray-brown head and an airfoil-shaped white patch behind her eye. Flight is low to the water with rapid wing beats. The illustration shows a breeding male, below, and a female, above.

Ruddy Duck, *Oxyura jamaicencis*
Family Anatidae (Ducks and Geese)
Size: 15"
Range: Throughout Florida; winter
Habitat: Open water, fresh- or saltwater wetlands

The ruddy duck is a member of the "stiff-tailed ducks," known for rigid tail feathers that are often cocked up in display. The ruddy duck dives deep into the water for aquatic vegetation, and flies low over the water with quick wing beats. It is a relatively small duck with a big head and a flat, broad body. The breeding male is a rich sienna brown overall, with white cheeks, a black cap and nape, and a bright blue bill. The female is drab, with a conspicuous dark stripe across the cheek. Nonbreeding males become gray. The ruddy duck can sink low into the water, grebelike, and will often dive to escape danger. The illustration shows a breeding male, below, and a female, above.

American Flamingo, *Phoenicopterus ruber*
Family Phoenicopteridae (Flamingos)
Size: 48"
Range: Southern and central Florida; winter
Habitat: Saltwater flats and the Florida Keys

The rare American flamingo walks slowly and steadily through the shallows with its head upside down in the water, moving it from side to side to extract small aquatic prey and shrimp. It is unmistakable, with a pink body, black wings, extremely long legs and neck, and a thick, two-toned bill that bends down at its midpoint. Flamingos run to take off and often fly in flocks forming long, single-file lines in the sky, emitting honking calls. Young flamingos are very pale with gray on the back; they gradually acquire the pink plumage. The illustration shows an adult.

White-tailed Tropicbird, *Phaethon lepturus*
Family Phaethontidae (Tropicbirds)
Size: 30"
Range: Coastal Florida; spring and summer
Habitat: Open coastal waters

The white-tailed tropicbird is graceful, tern-shaped, and often seen soaring high up. To feed, it drops from the heights and plunge-dives for fish and squid. Its plumage is white with contrasting black patches at the base of the primaries and long oblique black stripes along the inner wing. The head has a dark eye line and the bill is yellow-orange. The extremely long and delicate inner tail feathers are conspicuous; they are lacking in the juvenile. Florida is the only reliable place to see this bird in the United States. The illustration shows an adult.

Wood Stork, *Mycteria americana*
Family Ciconiidae (Storks)
Size: 40"
Range: Throughout Florida; year-round
Habitat: Open saltwater or freshwater marshes

The wood stork is large and somewhat unattractive, with a white body, black flight feathers, and a featherless neck and head covered in blackish, scaly skin. The bill is long, decurved, and blunt at its tip. It feeds by probing its bill into the mud, stirring up prey such as fish and snakes, and flies with its neck outstretched. Storks fly in loose, unorganized groups. At rest the wood stork will stand motionless for an hour or more in a distinctive, upright posture with its bill tucked down and against its body. The stork roosts in mangrove or cypress trees, and emits croaking sounds or chatters by snapping the upper and lower mandibles together. The illustration shows an adult.

Magnificent Frigatebird, *Fregata magnificens*
Family Fregatidae (Frigatebirds)
Size: 40"
Range: Coastal Florida; year-round
Habitat: Coastal waters and the southern Keys

The magnificent frigatebird can be seen soaring effortlessly for hours, high above the coast. To feed, it skims the surface of the water in flight to snatch fish, or may steal food from other seabirds. It has long slender wings and a deeply forked tail. The bill is long and hooked. Males are black overall, with a curious red throat patch that can be inflated like a balloon. Females have white bellies and sides. The illustration shows an adult female.

Double-crested Cormorant, *Phalacrocorax auritus*
Family Phalacrocoracidae (Cormorants)
Size: 32"
Range: Throughout Florida; year-round
Habitat: Open expanses of freshwater or salt water

Named for the two long, white plumes that emerge behind its eyes during breeding season, the double-crested cormorant is an expert swimmer that dives underwater to chase down fish. Because its plumage lacks the normal oils that repel water, it will stand with wings outstretched to dry. It is all black with a pale, glossy cast to the back and wings. The eye is bright green, the bill thin and hooked, and the throat patch and lores are yellow. The illustration shows a breeding adult.

Anhinga, *Anhinga anhinga*
Family Anhingidae (Anhinga)
Size: 34"
Range: Throughout Florida; year-round
Habitat: Freshwater ponds and swamps

With a cormorantlike body and snakelike neck, the anhinga swims underwater to spear fish with its sharp, daggerlike bill. It may be seen with only its head above water, or soaring high above the marshes. The anhinga will often stand with wings outstretched to dry. Its body is black with finely patterned white streaks; its tail is long, barred with white and tipped with brown. The female has a pale brown neck and head, while the head and neck of the male are all black. In breeding plumage, the male develops an upturned crest. The illustration shows an adult female.

43

Brown Pelican, *Pelecanus occidentalis*
Family Pelecanidae (Pelicans)
Size: 50"
Range: Coastal Florida; year-round
Habitat: Near-shore coastal waters

The majestic brown pelican enlivens coastal waters with its spectacular feeding process of plunge-diving for fish, headfirst, from some height. In flight, pelicans often cruise in formation inches from incoming swells, gaining lift and rarely needing to flap their wings. The plumage is bleached gray-brown overall, with a white head and neck and a massive bill. When breeding, the head is pale yellow with a brown-red nape patch and a black strip down the back of the neck. Quite gregarious, the pelican may nest in mangrove trees or in slight depressions in the sand or rocks. The illustration shows a breeding adult.

Great Blue Heron, *Ardea herodias*
Family Ardeidae (Herons and Egrets)
Size: 46"
Range: Throughout Florida; year-round
Habitat: Most aquatic areas, including lakes, creeks, and marshes

The great blue heron is the largest heron in North America. Walking slowly through shallow water or fields, it stalks fish, crabs, and small vertebrates with the help of its massive bill. With long legs and neck, it is blue-gray overall, with a white face and a heavy, yellow-orange bill. The crown is black and supports plumes of medium length. The front of the neck is white, with distinct black chevrons fading into the breast plumes. In flight, the neck is tucked back and wing beats are regular and labored. The illustration shows an adult.

Great Egret, *Ardea alba*
Family Ardeidae (Herons and Egrets)
Size: 38"
Range: Throughout Florida; year-round
Habitat: Freshwater or saltwater marshes

One of North America's most widespread herons, the great egret is all white with a long, thin, yellow bill and long black legs. It develops long lacy plumes across its back during the breeding season. Stalking slowly, it pursues fish, frogs, and other aquatic animals. The illustration is a breeding adult.

Reddish Egret, *Egretta rufescens*
Family Ardeidae (Herons and Egrets)
Size: 26"
Range: Coastal Florida; year-round
Habitat: Coastal lagoons and mangroves

The reddish egret is thick-necked and has two color morphs: an all-white version and the more common dark version. The dark morph is gray, with a rusty reddish neck lined with stringy coarse feathers that give the heron a disheveled look. The bill is long, powerful, and pinkish with a black tip. A quite active bird, the heron often runs through the shallows chasing after fish like a maniac. It also employs the technique of creating an area of shade with its outstretched wings to attract fish, enabling it to see them better. The bird is usually solitary. The illustration shows an adult.

Tricolored Heron, *Egretta tricolor*
Family Ardeidae (Herons and Egrets)
Size: 26"
Range: Throughout Florida; year-round
Habitat: Salt marshes, mangrove swamps

The tricolored heron is thin and bluish gray, with a white belly and a brownish neck stripe and lower back. In nonbreeding plumage it has yellow lores and an orangey bill, but in the breeding season the lores and bill are blue, and the bill has a dark tip. The heron also develops plumes behind the ears and across the lower back. To feed, it actively pursues prey or stands motionless, waiting to stab a fish or frog with its thin, spearlike bill. The illustration shows a breeding adult.

Green Heron, *Butorides virescens*
Family Ardeidae (Herons and Egrets)
Size: 18"
Range: Throughout Florida; year-round
Habitat: Ponds, creeks and coastal wetlands (freshwater or saltwater)

The green heron is compact and the size of a crow. It perches on low branches over the water, crouching forward to search for fish, snails, and insects. It is known to toss a bug into the water to help attract fish. The green heron is really not so green, but a dull grayish blue with a burgundy-chestnut neck and black crown. The bill is dark and the legs are bright yellow-orange. When disturbed, it will erect its crest feathers, stand erect, and twitch its tail. It is fairly secretive and solitary. The illustration shows an adult.

Black-crowned Night Heron, *Nycticorax nycticorax*
Family Ardeidae (Herons and Egrets)
Size: 25"
Range: Throughout Florida; year-round
Habitat: Marshes, swamps with wooded banks

The nocturnal black-crowned night heron is stocky and thick-necked, with a comparatively large head and a sharp, heavy, thick bill. It has pale gray wings, white underparts, and a black crown, back, and bill. Its eyes are piercing red and its legs are yellow. When breeding, the night heron develops long, white plumes on the rear of the head. During the day the heron roosts in groups, but at night it forages alone, waiting motionless for prey such as fish or crabs. It may even raid the nests of other birds for their young. Its voice is composed of low-pitched barks and croaks. The illustration shows an adult.

White Ibis, *Eudocimus albus*
Family Threskiornithidae (Ibises and Spoonbills)
Size: 25"
Range: Throughout Florida; year-round
Habitat: Salt marshes, swamps, mangroves, fields

Fairly common in southern Florida, the white ibis forages in groups, probing mud and shallow water for small aquatic animals and invertebrates. It is all white except for the black tips of its primaries, which are rarely visible unless the wings are outstretched. The long, downward-curved bill is red with a darker tip, and meets unfeathered, reddish-pink facial skin that reaches to the eye. Its legs are red. The juvenile is dark brown above, with a dark, streaky neck. Ibises fly with their necks outstretched, unlike herons, which fly with their necks folded back. The illustration shows an adult.

Roseate Spoonbill, *Platalea ajaja*
Family Threskiornithidae (Ibises and Spoonbills)
Size: 32"
Range: Southern Florida; year-round
Habitat: Shallow saltwater wetlands, mangrove marshes, agricultural fields

The roseate spoonbill is easily identified by its unique feeding technique. It swings its bill from side to side in shallow water or mud to catch fish, shrimp, and other small aquatic life. Unlike the heron, it constantly moves forward and seldom remains stationary. Its body is pink with red in the shoulders; its neck is white and tail is orange. Its face is pale green-gray bordered by a black feathered patch. The bill is very long, thick at the base then thinning to a compressed spatula shape. The spoonbill flies with its neck outstretched. While resting, it will stand on one leg for considerable lengths of time. The illustration shows an adult.

Snail Kite, *Rostrhamus sociabilis*
Family Accipitridae (Hawks and Eagles)
Size: 17"
Range: Central and southern Florida; year-round
Habitat: Freshwater marshes

Also known as the Everglade kite, the snail kite is a tropical species with very specific feeding habits. It relies almost exclusively on a certain "apple snail" that it snatches from the grass while in flight. It then removes the flesh from the snail shell with its sharply hooked bill and sharp talons. The plumage is dark overall, except for the front half of the tail, which is white. Males are dark slate gray with red legs. Females are dark brown with a streaked breast and lighter facial markings. Florida is the only US state in which the snail kite is found, and its numbers are very sensitive to habitat changes and the availability of snails. The illustration shows a male, below, and a female, above.

Swallow-tailed Kite, *Elanoides forficatus*
Family Accipitridae (Hawks and Eagles)
Size: 23"
Range: Throughout Florida; summer
Habitat: Wooded environments and wetlands

The swallow-tailed kite is a graceful, skilled flier that feeds on the wing, catching insects midair or snatching reptiles from tree branches. It even drinks by skimming along the water surface. The kite resembles a large swallow, with a long, deeply forked tail and long, thin wings. The body and head are white, and the back, tail, and wings are black. The bill is small and hooked, and the eye is dark. These kites may flock together while feeding or during migration to and from their winter home in South America. The illustration shows an adult.

Short-tailed Hawk, *Buteo brachyurus*
Family Accipitridae (Hawks and Eagles)
Size: 16"
Range: Central and southern Florida; year-round
Habitat: Forest or mixed woodland/grassland

The reclusive short-tailed hawk is a smallish, plump buteo with rounded wings and a short tail. The slim forehead runs contiguous with the upper bill, giving a flat-headed appearance. Two color morphs exist: The dark morph, more common in Florida, is dark brown overall with light wing linings, and the light morph has clean white underparts. In flight, this hawk holds its wings flat with the tips bending up. To feed, it kites above the treetops and plunges to capture prey. Florida is the only state in the country in which this tropical species is found. The illustration shows an adult dark morph.

Crested Caracara, *Caracara cheriway*
Family Falconidae (Falcons)
Size: 23"
Range: Central and southern Florida; year-round
Habitat: Dry prairies and scrubland

The crested caracara is a falcon that is somewhat vulturelike in its behavior. It forages on carcasses or immobile prey, which it finds by soaring on flat wings or cruising over pastures and open savanna. It may also perch on poles or on the ground. Its head seems large for its body and it has a long neck and long legs. It is, overall, a dark bird, with a white neck, black cap, and large, hooked bill. The face has a large patch of bare reddish skin. In flight the crested caracara's white wing tips and tail are distinctive. This tropical falcon is rare in the United States and was once a threatened species here. The illustration shows an adult.

American Kestrel, *Falco sparverius*
Family Falconidae (Falcons)
Size: 10"
Range: Throughout Florida; year-round
Habitat: Branches or wires in open country and urban areas

Our most common falcon, the American kestrel, is a robin-size falcon with long, pointed wings and tail, and fast flight. It hovers above fields or dives from its perch to capture small animals and insects. Its upper parts are rufous-barred with black, its wings are blue-gray, and its breast is buff-colored or white-streaked with black spots. The head is patterned with a gray crown and vertical patches of black down the face. The female has rufous wings and a barred tail. Also known as the sparrow hawk, the kestrel has a habit of flicking its tail up and down while perched. The illustration shows an adult male.

Common Moorhen, *Gallinula chloropus*
Family Rallidae (Rails and Coots)
Size: 14"
Range: Throughout Florida; year-round
Habitat: Freshwater ponds and wetlands

The common moorhen, like the coot, is actually a type of rail that behaves more like a duck. It paddles along, bobbing its head up and down, picking at the water surface for any small aquatic animals, insects, or plants. Having short wings it is a poor flier, but its very long toes allow it to walk on floating vegetation. The moorhen is overall dark gray with a brownish back, black head, and white areas on the tail and sides. In breeding plumage, the forehead shield is deep red and the bill is red with a yellow tip. The moorhen is also known as the common gallinule. The illustration shows a breeding adult.

Limpkin, *Aramus guarauna*
Family Aramidae (Limpkins)
Size: 26"
Range: Central and southern Florida; year-round
Habitat: Shallow wetlands with vegetation

Named for its slow walking gait, which resembles a limp, the limpkin looks somewhat like a small crane. It has a long neck, long legs, and a long, decurving bill. Its plumage is dark brown with white streaking down the head and neck and onto the front half of the body. In flight it holds its neck extended below its body, creating a humpbacked appearance. Limpkins forage by walking steadily through shallow water or by swimming, picking out mollusks, apple snails, and other aquatic invertebrates. Its voice is a loud, raucous call. The illustration shows an adult.

Sandhill Crane, *Grus canadensis*
Family Gruidae (Cranes)
Size: 45"
Range: Throughout Florida; year-round
Habitat: Fields, shallow wetlands, and savanna

The sandhill crane is tall bird with long, strong legs, a long neck, and a long, straight bill. Long, thick tertial feathers create the distinctive bustle on the rears of all cranes. The top of the sandhill crane's head is covered in red, bare skin. Its plumage is gray overall, but may become spotted with rust-colored stains by preening with a bill stained by iron-rich mud. Feeding in flocks, the crane grazes in fields, gleaning grains, insects, and small animals, returning in the evening to roost in protected wetland areas. The voice of the sandhill crane is a throaty, penetrating, trumpeting sound. Unlike the heron, it flies in groups with its neck extended. The Florida population is non-migratory and larger than northern populations. The illustration shows an adult.

Semipalmated Plover, *Charadrius semipalmatus*
Family Charadriidae (Plovers)
Size: 7"
Range: Throughout Florida; mostly in winter
Habitat: Open sand or mudflats, coastal beaches

The semipalmated plover is small and plump, with pointed wings, large black eyes, and a relatively large, rounded head. It has a dark brown back and crown, is white below, and has a small, orange bill with a dark tip. The head has dark bands across the eye and encircling the neck. Its legs and feet are yellow. Winter and breeding plumages are similar, with the exception of an all dark bill and lighter supercilium in winter. Semipalmated plovers are widespread and fly in flocks, but they disperse to feed, using fast running interrupted by sudden stops to probe for invertebrates. The bird's name is derived from the partial webbing at the base of its toes. The illustration shows a breeding adult.

Killdeer, *Charadrius vociferus*
Family Charadriidae (Plovers)
Size: 10"
Range: Throughout Florida; year-round
Habitat: Inland fields, farmlands, lake shores, and meadows

The killdeer gets its name from the piercing *kill-dee* call that you often hear before seeing this well-camouflaged plover. Well adapted to human-altered environments, the killdeer is quite widespread and gregarious. It has long, pointed wings, a long tail, and a conspicuous double-banded breast. Its upper parts are dark brown, its belly is white, and its head is patterned with a white supercilium and forehead. The tail is rusty orange with a black tip. There is a noticeable white stripe across the flight feathers when the bird is in flight. The killdeer is known for the classic "broken wing" display, which it uses to distract predators from its nest and young. The illustration shows an adult.

American Oystercatcher, *Haematopus palliatus*
Family Haematopodidae (Oystercatchers)
Size: 18"
Range: Throughout Florida; year-round
Habitat: Coastal beaches and tide pools

The American oystercatcher is a chunky, short-tailed, and short-winged shorebird with a dark brown back, white belly, and black head. It has a heavy, knifelike, bright red bill, yellow eyes, and stocky, salmon-colored legs. When in flight, a distinct white bar is visible across the secondary feathers. The oystercatcher follows the tidal pattern, foraging at low tide and roosting at high tide in groups with other shorebirds and gulls. It uses its bill to pry shellfish—including oysters—away from rocks, or to probe for worms. The bill is also used to jam open bivalves and devour their flesh. Its voice is a loud, piping call. The illustration shows an adult.

Black-necked Stilt, *Himantopus mexicanus*
Family Recurvirostridae (Avocets and Stilts)
Size: 14"
Range: Throughout Florida; year-round
Habitat: Shallow wetlands, marshes, and lagoons

The black-necked stilt literally looks like a tiny body on stilts. It has extremely long, delicate, red legs and a thin, straight, needlelike black bill. Its wings and mantle are black, and its underparts and tail are white. The head is dark above, with a white patch above the eye. The female has a slightly lighter, brownish back. In flight its long legs dangle behind the bird. To forage, the stilt strides along, picking small prey from the water or vegetation, and may voice a strident, barking *kek* in alarm. Stilts are also known to perform the broken-wing or broken-leg act to distract predators. The illustration shows an adult male.

Willet, *Tringa semipalmata*
Family Scolopacidae (Sandpipers and Phalaropes)
Size: 15"
Range: Throughout Florida; year-round
Habitat: Saltwater or freshwater wetlands, coastlines

The willet is a heavy shorebird with a stout bill and conspicuous black-and-white wing markings in flight. It has overall mocha-brown plumage above and is pale below, with extensive mottling in the breeding season. It has white lores and eye rings, and its plain gray legs are thick and sturdy. It is found singly or in scattered flocks, and picks or probes for crabs, crustaceans, and worms in the mud and sand. Its call is a loud *wil-let*, often uttered in flight. The illustration shows a nonbreeding adult.

Sanderling, *Calidris alba*
Family Scolopacidae (Sandpipers and Phalaropes)
Size: 8"
Range: Throughout Florida; mostly in winter
Habitat: Coastal beaches and mudflats

The sanderling is a common shorebird that runs back and forth following the incoming and outgoing surf, grabbing invertebrates exposed by the waves. It is a small, active, squat sandpiper with a short bill and legs. In nonbreeding plumage, it is very pale above and white below, which contrasts with its black legs and bill. There is a distinct black shoulder and leading edge on the wing. Females in breeding plumage are speckled brown above, while males develop rufous coloring on the back, head, and neck. A white wing stripe on the upper wing can be seen when the bird is in flight. Sanderlings may form large foraging flocks, and even larger flocks while roosting. The illustration shows a nonbreeding adult.

Laughing Gull, *Leucophaeus atricilla*
Family Laridae (Gulls and Terns)
Size: 16"
Range: Throughout Florida; year-round
Habitat: Coastal beaches and marshes, urban environments, pastures

The laughing gull is so named because of its loud, often incessant, laughing squawk, and it is the only gull known to breed in Florida. Social and uninhibited, it is a relatively thin, medium-size gull with long, pointed wings. The breeding adult has a black head with white eye arcs and a dark red bill. Its upper parts are dark gray, the underparts are white, and the wing tips are black with small white dots at the end. The nonbreeding adult has a white head with faint dark smudging behind the eye. Laughing gulls eat crabs, fish, and worms, and will scavenge from humans for food or even steal from other birds. The illustration shows a breeding adult, below, and a nonbreeding adult, above.

Herring Gull, *Larus argentatus*
Family Laridae (Gulls and Terns)
Size: 25"
Range: Throughout Florida; winter
Habitat: Mainly coastal but may travel inland; beaches, harbors, fields

The widespread herring gull occurs across the North American continent. It is a large, relatively thin, white-headed gull with a pale gray back and white underparts. The bill is thick and yellow, with a reddish spot at the tip of the lower mandible. The primaries are black with white-spotted tips. The nonbreeding adult has brown streaking across the nape and neck. The legs are pink and the eye is pale yellow to ivory. The herring gull is an opportunistic feeder, eating fish, worms, crumbs, and trash. It is known to drop shellfish from the air to crack open the shells. The illustration shows a breeding adult, below, and a nonbreeding adult, above.

Royal Tern, *Thalasseus maximus*
Family Laridae (Gulls and Terns)
Size: 20"
Range: Throughout Florida; year-round
Habitat: Coastal beaches, salt marshes

The royal tern is large and sleek, with thin, pointed wings, a black, crested cap, and a pointed red-orange bill. It is pale gray above and white below, with black legs. The nonbreeding adult has limited dark coloring on its head, often reduced to a dark patch just behind the eye. The dark outer primaries are visible in flight. Like the Caspian tern, the royal tern flies over the water surface, often hovering, and then plunges down to catch fish. It breeds on sandbars in the company of thousands of other birds. The illustration shows a breeding adult, below, and a nonbreeding adult, above.

Least Tern, *Sternula antillarum*
Family Laridae (Gulls and Terns)
Size: 9"
Range: Throughout Florida; summer
Habitat: Sandy coastal shores, wetlands

The least tern is the smallest North American tern and the only tern with a yellow bill and legs. It has a black cap and a white forehead patch, and is pale gray above and white below. The tail is forked, and the bill tipped with black. Nonbreeding adults have a dark bill and more white on the front of the cap. In flight the tern's wings are relatively narrow, and there is a black bar on the outer primaries. Least terns often hover over the water before plunge-diving to catch small fish. They also pick worms and insects from the ground. This sensitive bird was once threatened by development on its sandy coastal breeding grounds. The illustration shows a breeding adult.

Black Skimmer, *Rynchops niger*
Family Laridae (Gulls and Terns)
Size: 18"
Range: Coastal Florida; year-round
Habitat: Coastal bays, estuaries, and inland freshwater rivers and lakes

The black skimmer has a most unique bill in that the lower mandible is substantially longer than the upper. The red bill is also thick at the base and knife-thin toward the end. This aids in the bird's foraging practice of flying just above the water surface, wings held above its body, with its mouth open and the lower mandible cutting a furrow through the water. When the skimmer encounters something solid, its mouth slams shut and, hopefully, the bird acquires a fish. Its plumage is black on the back, wings, and crown, and white below. The legs are tiny and red. Nonbreeding adults have a white nape, contiguous with the white of the body. The illustration shows a breeding adult.

Mourning Dove, *Zenaida macroura*
Family Columbidae (Pigeons and Doves)
Size: 12"
Range: Throughout Florida; year-round
Habitat: Open brushy areas and urban areas

The common mourning dove is sleek and long-tailed, with a thin neck, a small, rounded head, and a large black eye. It is pale gray-brown underneath and darker above, with some iridescence to the feathers on the neck. There are distinct black spots on the tertials and some coverts, and a dark spot on the upper neck below the eye. The pointed tail is edged with a white band. The mourning dove pecks on the ground for seeds and grains, and walks with quick, short steps while bobbing its head. Flight is strong and direct, and the dove's wings create a whistle as it takes off. Its voice is a mournful, owl-like cooing. It is usually solitary or found in small groups, but may form large flocks where food is abundant. The illustration shows an adult.

White-crowned Pigeon, *Patagioenas leucocephala*
Family Columbidae (Pigeons and Doves)
Size: 13"
Range: Southern Florida and the Keys; year-round
Habitat: Forested areas, mangroves

The white-crowned pigeon is a Caribbean species that is rare and threatened in Florida. It forages among trees for seeds and fruit, voicing its deep, cooing call. It is a large pigeon with short, rounded wings. The body is a dark slate gray. It has a white crown extending just below the white eye, and its nape is barred with iridescent feathers. The bill is red with a pale tip. In juvenile pigeons, the white cap is absent. The illustration shows an adult.

Mangrove Cuckoo, *Coccyzus minor*
Family Cuculidae (Cuckoos)
Size: 12"
Range: South and central Florida; year-round
Habitat: Mangrove forests, hardwood hammocks, and scrub

The shy mangrove cuckoo skulks among trees picking out insects and caterpillars while voicing a nasal call of *gaw-gaw-gaw-gaw*. It is brown above and whitish to cinnamon-buff below, and the gray cap on its head is darkest just behind the eye. Its bill is two-toned, with the upper mandible gray and the lower mandible yellow. The underside of the long, gradated tail is black with big white spots. The illustration shows an adult.

Smooth-billed Ani, *Crotophaga ani*
Family Cuculidae (Cuckoos)
Size: 14"
Range: Central and southern Florida; year-round
Habitat: Open fields, grasslands, urban areas

The fairly rare but social smooth-billed ani is a scruffy, grackle-size black bird that often appears hunched or holds its wings and tail at odd angles. Its bill is large and laterally compressed, with the top mandible being much larger that the lower, and with a thin keel at the top edge. Plumage is black, tinged brown on the head and neck and blue-green along the back, wings, and tail. The ani picks insects, fruit, and small reptiles or amphibians from the ground or branches. Its call is a questioning *wa-eek?* The illustration shows an adult.

Great Horned Owl, *Bubo virginianus*
Family Strigidae (Owls)
Size: 22"
Range: Throughout Florida; year-round
Habitat: Found in almost any environment; forests to plains to urban areas

Ranging throughout North America, the great horned owl is large and strong, with an obvious facial disk and sharp, long talons. Plumage is variable, but the eastern form is brown overall, with heavy barring, a rust-colored face, and a white chin patch. The prominent ear tufts give the owl its name, and the eyes are large and yellow. The great horned owl has exceptional hearing and sight. It feeds at night, perching on branches or posts and then swooping down on silent wings to catch birds, snakes, or mammals up to the size of a cat. Its voice is a low *hoo-hoo-hoo*. The illustration shows an adult.

Burrowing Owl, *Athene cunicularia*
Family Strigidae (Owls)
Size: 9.5"
Range: Throughout Florida; year-round
Habitat: Open grasslands and plains

The burrowing owl is ground-dwelling, living in burrows that have been vacated by rodents or tortoises. It is small, flat-headed, and has a short tail and long legs. Plumage is brown above, spotted with white, and extensively barred brown and white below. The owl has a white chin and throat, and bright yellow eyes. The Florida variety is darker and more barred than its western counterparts. Burrowing owls can be seen day or night, perched on the ground or a post and scanning for insects and small rodents. Sometimes the owl exhibits a bowing movement when approached. The burrowing owl's voice is a chattering or cooing, and sometimes imitative of a rattlesnake. The illustration shows an adult.

Chuck-will's-widow, *Caprimulgus carolinensis*
Family Caprimulgidae (Nightjars and Nighthawks)
Size: 12"
Range: Throughout Florida; year-round
Habitat: Woodland areas with clearings

Chuck-will's-widow is a fairly large, highly camouflaged nightjar with a fat head, big dark eyes, and a tiny bill. Its body is thick and broad around the midsection, giving the bird a hunched appearance. It is overall rusty or brown-gray, spotted and streaked with black. There are pale edges to the scapulars and a pale chin stripe above the dark breast. The tail is long and projects beyond the primaries. In flight you can see the long, pointed wings and white on the outer tail feathers in the males. Chuck-will's-widows are nocturnal, feeding at night by springing from a perch or from the ground for flying insects. During the day the bird roosts on the ground or in trees with its eyes closed. Its voice is somewhat like its name, *chuck-wil-wi-dow*. The illustration shows an adult.

Chimney Swift, *Chaetura pelagica*
Family Apodidae (Swifts)
Size: 5"
Range: Throughout Florida; summer
Habitat: Found in a variety of environments, including woods, scrub, swamps, and urban areas

The gregarious chimney swift is unrelated to swallows but is similar in shape. Its body is like a fat torpedo, with a very short tail and long, pointed, bowed wings that bend close to the body. It is dark brown overall, and slightly paler underneath and at the chin. Constantly on the wing, it catches insects in flight with quick wing beats and fast glides. It never perches, but roosts at night on vertical cliffs, on trees, or in chimneys. Its voice is a quick chattering uttered in flight. The illustration shows an adult.

Ruby-throated Hummingbird, *Archilochus colubris*
Family Trochilidae (Hummingbirds)
Size: 3.5"
Range: Throughout Florida; mostly summer but year-round in southern Florida
Habitat: Areas with flowering plants, including gardens and at urban feeders

The ruby-throated hummingbird is small, delicate, and able to hover on wings that beat at a blinding speed. The long, needle-like bill is used to probe deep into flowers so the bird can lap up the nectar. Its feet are tiny, and its body is white below and green above. Males have a dark green crown and iridescent red throat (gorget). Females lack the colored gorget, and have a light green crown and white-tipped tail feathers. The bird's behavior is typi-cal of hummingbirds, hovering and buzzing from flower to flower, emitting chits and squeaks. Most of these birds migrate across the Gulf of Mexico to South America in the winter. The illustration shows an adult male, below, and female, above.

Belted Kingfisher, *Megaceryle alcyon*
Family Alcedinidae (Kingfishers)
Size: 13"
Range: Throughout Florida; year-round
Habitat: Creeks, lakes, sheltered coastlines

The widespread but solitary belted kingfisher is a stocky, large-headed bird with a long, powerful bill and shaggy crest. It is gray-ish blue-green above and white below, with a thick blue band across the breast and white dotting on the back. A white spot is at the lores. The female has an extra rufous breast band and is rufous along the flanks. Belted kingfishers feed by springing from a perch along the water's edge, or by hovering above the water and then plunging headfirst to snatch fish, frogs, and tadpoles. Its flight is uneven and its voice is a raspy, rattling sound. The illustration shows an adult female.

Downy Woodpecker, *Picoides pubescens*
Family Picidae (Woodpeckers)
Size: 6.5"
Range: Throughout Florida; year-round
Habitat: Woodlands, parks, urban areas, stream sides

The downy woodpecker is tiny, with a small bill and a relatively large head. It is white underneath with no barring, has black wings barred with white, and has a patch of white on its back. The head is boldly patterned white and black, and the male sports a red nape patch. The base of the bill joins the head with fluffy nasal tufts. Juveniles may show some red on the forehead and crown. The downy woodpecker forages for berries and insects in the bark and smaller twigs of trees. The very similar hairy woodpecker is larger, with a longer bill and more aggressive foraging behavior, sticking to larger branches and not clinging to twigs. The illustration shows an adult male.

Pileated Woodpecker, *Dryocopus pileatus*
Family Picidae (Woodpeckers)
Size: 16.5"
Range: Throughout Florida; year-round
Habitat: Old-growth forests, urban areas with large trees

The pileated woodpecker is North America's largest woodpecker, except for the huge ivory-billed woodpecker, which is probably extinct. The pileated woodpecker is very large, powerful, long-necked, and crested. The body is all black with a white base on the primaries, which are mostly covered in the folded wing. The head is boldly patterned black and white, with a bright red crest that is limited on the female. The male has a red malar patch instead of the black of the female. In flight the contrasting white wing lining can be seen. To forage, pileated woodpeckers chip away chunks of bark to uncover ants and beetles, but will feed on berries during winter months. The woodpecker's voice is a high-pitched, uneven, resounding *wok-wok-wok*. The illustration shows an adult male.

Red-bellied Woodpecker, *Melanerpes carolinus*
Family Picidae (Woodpeckers)
Size: 9"
Range: Throughout Florida; year-round
Habitat: Woodlands, wooded swamps, parks, urban areas

The red-bellied woodpecker is fairly common. It is large-billed, with an extensively barred back and wings. Its underparts are pale buff, with a barely discernable hint of rose on the belly that gives the bird its name. The crown and nape are reddish orange in males. Females lack the red crown, and juveniles have an entirely gray head. Like all woodpeckers, the red-bellied woodpecker has two toes pointing forward and two pointing back to allow a secure grip on a tree trunk as it pecks away bark to find insects. It also feeds on nuts and oranges. Its flight consists of undulating wing beats and glides. The illustration shows an adult male.

Red-cockaded Woodpecker, *Picoides borealis*
Family Picidae (Woodpeckers)
Size: 8.5"
Range: Throughout Florida; year-round
Habitat: Old-growth pine forests

The red-cockaded woodpecker nests only in mature pine trees; it is rare and declining in numbers as it loses habitat to development. It is a thin-looking, medium-size woodpecker with a long tail. Plumage is barred black and white on the back, and is white beneath, with numerous spots and bars. The patterned head has a large white cheek patch and nasal tufts. The red cockade at the back of the crown on the male is rarely apparent in the field. Juveniles show a red forehead spot. This bird forms small groups called clans that forage together, pecking into tree bark for beetles and other insects. The illustration shows an adult male.

Red-headed Woodpecker, *Melanerpes erythrocephalus*
Family Picidae (Woodpeckers)
Size: 9"
Range: Throughout Florida; year-round
Habitat: Woodlands, areas with standing dead trees, suburbs

The red-headed woodpecker has a striking bright red head and a powerful, tapered bill. It is black above, with a large patch of white across the lower back and secondaries, and is white below. The juvenile has a pale brown head and an incomplete white back patch. In all woodpeckers the tail is very stiff, with sharp tips to support the bird while it clings to a tree trunk. To feed, it pecks at tree bark to uncover insects, but may also fly out to snatch its prey in midair. Nuts will also be taken and stored in tree cavities for winter. This species has been losing nesting cavities to the European starling since that bird's introduction. The illustration shows an adult.

BIRDS: PASSERINES

Great Crested Flycatcher, *Myiarchus crinitus*
Family Tyrannidae (Tyrant Flycatchers)
Size: 8.5"
Range: Throughout Florida; year-round
Habitat: Open woodlands and scrub, urban areas

The great crested flycatcher is large, with a proportionately large head and full crest. The upper parts and head are olive-brown, the throat and breast are gray, and the belly is bright yellow. The primaries and tail show rufous color, while the margins to the tertials and coverts are white. Both sexes and the juvenile are similar in plumage. In flight the yellow wing linings and rufous tail may be noted. The flycatcher feeds by catching insects in flight between perches. It is often seen erecting its crown feathers and bobbing its head. Its voice is a high-pitched, whistling *wheeeerup!* The illustration shows an adult.

Eastern Kingbird, *Tyrannus tyrannus*
Family Tyrannidae (Tyrant Flycatchers)
Size: 8.5"
Range: Throughout Florida; summer
Habitat: Open woodlands, agricultural and rural areas

The eastern kingbird is a slender, medium-size flycatcher. Its upper parts are bluish black, and its underparts are white, with a pale gray breast. The dark head cap contrasts with the white lower half of the face. The tail is black with a white terminal band. The eastern kingbird flies with shallow wing beats on wings that are mostly dark and pointed. It perches on wires, treetops, or posts, and takes flight to capture insects on the wing. Its voice is a distinctive series of very high-pitched, sputtering, zippy, *psit* notes. The illustration shows an adult.

Loggerhead Shrike, *Lanius ludovicianus*
Family Laniidae (Shrikes)
Size: 9.5"
Range: Throughout Florida; year-round
Habitat: Open, dry country with available perches including branches, wires, and posts

The solitary loggerhead shrike is raptorlike in its feeding habits. It captures large insects, small mammals, and birds and impales them on thorny barbs before tearing them apart to feed. It is a compact, large-headed bird with a short, thick, slightly hooked bill. Its upper parts are gray and underparts are pale. Its wings are black, with white patches at the bases of the primaries and upper coverts. Its tail is black and edged with white. There is a black mask on the head from the base of the bill to the ear area. Juveniles show a finely barred breast. The shrike's flight is composed of quick wing beats and swooping glides. The illustration shows an adult.

Yellow-throated Vireo, *Vireo flavifrons*
Family Vireonidae (Vireos)
Size: 5.5"
Range: Throughout Florida; year-round
Habitat: High canopy in mature, moist, mixed woodlands

The yellow-throated vireo is compact, with a short tail. It has olive and gray upper parts, with a bright yellow chin and breast fading to a white belly and undertail region. Yellow "spectacles" encompass the dark eyes. There are two distinct white wing bars on the wing coverts. This vireo gleans insects and berries from leaves high in the canopy. The illustration shows an adult.

Florida Scrub Jay, *Aphelocoma coerulescens*
Family Corvidae (Jays and Crows)
Size: 11"
Range: Most of Florida except for the Panhandle region; year-round
Habitat: Open scrub oak chaparral, urban areas

The Florida scrub jay is a rare bird, declining in numbers with the loss of habitat. It is a long-necked, sleek, crestless jay. Its upper parts are deep blue with a distinct, lighter gray-brown mantle. The underparts are pale gray and lightly streaked with brown. Its forehead is white, and its throat is streaked with white above a blue "necklace" across its breast. Its flight is made up of an undulating combination of rapid wing beats and swooping glides. Its food consists of nuts, seeds, insects, and fruit. The illustration shows an adult.

American Crow, *Corvus brachyrhynchos*
Family Corvidae (Jays and Crows)
Size: 17.5"
Range: Throughout Florida; year-round
Habitat: Open woodlands, pastures, rural fields, dumps

The American crow is a widespread corvid found across the continent, often heard voicing its familiar, loud, grating *caw, caw*. It is a large, stocky bird with a short, rounded tail, broad wings, and a thick, powerful bill. Plumage is overall glistening black. It will eat almost anything, and often forms loose flocks with other crows. The illustration shows an adult.

Northern Rough-winged Swallow, *Stelgidopteryx serripennis*
Family Hirundinidae (Swallows)
Size: 5.5"
Range: Throughout Florida; year-round
Habitat: Sandy cliffs, riverbanks, outcrops, bridges

The northern rough-winged swallow flies in a smooth and even
fashion with full wing beats and feeds on insects caught on the
fly. It is uniformly brownish above and white below. The breast is
lightly streaked with pale brown, and the tail is short and square.
Juveniles show light, rust-colored wing bars on the upper coverts.
These fairly solitary swallows find nesting sites in holes in sandy
cliffs. The illustration shows an adult.

Barn Swallow, *Hirundo rustica*
Family Hirundinidae (Swallows)
Size: 6.5"
Range: Throughout Florida; summer
Habitat: Open rural areas near bridges, as well as old buildings and caves

The widespread and common barn swallow has narrow, pointed wings and a long, deeply forked tail. It is pale below and dark blue above, with a rusty orange forehead and throat. In males the underparts are pale orange, while females are pale cream below. Barn swallows are graceful, fluid fliers, and they often forage in groups while catching insects in flight. The voice is a loud, repetitive chirping or clicking. Barn swallows build cup-shaped nests of mud on almost any protected man-made structure. The illustration shows an adult male.

Carolina Chickadee, *Poecile carolinensis*
Family Paridae (Chickadees and Titmice)
Size: 4.75"
Range: Throughout Florida; year-round
Habitat: Woodland areas, feeders

The Carolina chickadee is a small, compact, active bird with short rounded wings. It is gray above and lighter gray or dusky below, with a contrasting black cap and throat patch. It is quite similar to the black-capped chickadee, which does not normally occur in Florida. Its voice sounds like its name, *chick-a-dee, dee, dee,* or may be a soft *fee-bay*. The chickadee is quite social and feeds on a variety of seeds, berries, and insects found in trees and shrubs. The illustration shows an adult.

Brown-headed Nuthatch, *Sitta pusilla*
Family Sittidae (Nuthatches)
Size: 4.5"
Range: Northern Florida; year-round
Habitat: Pine woodlands

Clinging to tree trunks facing downward, the little brown-headed
nuthatch creeps down a tree picking insects, larvae, or seeds from
the bark. It is a compact, short-necked, large-headed bird with a
short stubby tail. Its legs are short, but its toes are long to help
grasp the bark. Its bill is long, thin, sharp, and upturned at the tip.
Its plumage is gray above and lighter gray or buff-colored below.
It has a brown cap, a dark eye line, and a small white spot on the
nape of its neck. The flight of the nuthatch is undulating. The birds
nest in cavities in tree trunks. The illustration shows an adult.

Marsh Wren, *Cistothorus palustris*
Family Troglodytidae (Wrens)
Size: 5"
Range: Throughout Florida; year-round
Habitat: Marshes, reeds, stream banks

The marsh wren is small, cryptic and rufous-brown with a normally cocked-up tail. Its tail and wings are barred with black, and the chin and breast are white. There is a well-defined white superciliary stripe below a uniform brown crown, and its mantle shows distinct black-and-white striping. The bird's bill is long and slightly decurved. Marsh wrens are vocal day and night, voicing quick, repetitive cheeping. They are secretive but inquisitive, and glean insects from marsh vegetation and the water surface. The illustration shows an adult.

Red-whiskered Bulbul, *Pycnonotus jocosus*
Family Pycnonotidae (Bulbuls)
Size: 7"
Range: Southern Florida; year-round
Habitat: Suburban gardens, parks with shrubs, agricultural areas

Introduced from Asia, the red-whiskered bulbul is a stocky bird with a long tail, an obvious pointed crest tuft, and a boldly patterned face. It is brown above and white below, with light brown sides and flanks. A dark arc crosses the breast and a thin dark stripe borders the lower face. Bright red "whiskers" emerge from behind the eye, and the undertail coverts are bright orange-red. The bulbul has short, rounded wings, and its flight is uneven. It forages on berries, fruit, and small insects. The illustration shows an adult.

American Robin, *Turdus migratorius*
Family Turdidae (Thrushes)
Size: 10"
Range: Throughout Florida; winter
Habitat: Widespread in a variety of environments, including woodlands, fields, parks, and lawns

Familiar and friendly, the American robin is a large thrush with a long tail and legs. It commonly holds its head cocked and wing tips lowered beneath its tail. It is gray-brown above and rufous below, with a darker head and contrasting white eye crescents and loral patches. The chin is streaked black and white, and the bill is yellow with darker edges. Females are typically paler over-all, and the juvenile shows spots of white above and dark below. Robins forage on the ground for earthworms and insects, or in trees to find berries. The song is a series of high, musical phrases like *cheery, cheer-up, cheerio*. The illustration shows an adult male.

Northern Mockingbird, *Mimus polyglottos*
Family Mimidae (Mockingbirds, Catbirds, and Thrashers)
Size: 10.5"
Range: Throughout Florida; year-round
Habitat: Open fields, grassy areas near vegetative cover, suburbs, parks

The northern mockingbird is the state bird of Florida. It is constantly vocalizing, and its scientific name, *polyglottos,* means "many voices," alluding to its amazing mimicry of the songs of other birds. It is sleek, long-tailed, and long-legged. Its plumage is gray above and off-white to brownish gray below, with darker wings and tail. The mockingbird sports two white wing bars, a short, dark, eye stripe, and a pale eye ring. In flight, the conspicuous white patch on the inner primaries and coverts, and white outer tail feathers, may be seen. Like other mimids, the bird forages on the ground for insects and berries, intermittently flicking its wings. The illustration shows an adult.

Northern Parula, *Parula americana*
Family Parulidae (Wood Warblers)
Size: 4.5"
Range: Throughout Florida; year-round
Habitat: Treetops in mossy woodlands

The northern parula is a tiny, stubby warbler with a short, sharp bill, short tail, and a relatively large head. Its upper parts are slate blue with a greenish mantle. Below is a white belly and under-tail. The parula has a yellow chin and breast, and a rufous breast band. Above and below the eyes are white eye arcs, and the lower mandible is yellow. The wings show two bold white wing bars. The female is bordered above the breast band with gray. Northern parulas forage for insects and caterpillars in trees. The illustration shows an adult male.

Hooded Warbler, *Wilsonia citrina*
Family Parulidae (Wood Warblers)
Size: 5"
Range: Throughout Florida; year-round except midwinter
Habitat: Moist woodlands, swamps

The hooded warbler lurks in the woodland understory, picking out insects while continually flicking its tail and singing its high, musical *weeta-weeta-weeta-toe*. Its plumage is olive green above and bright yellow below. The male has a full, black hood encompassing his face and chin, while the female has a fainter, partial mask with a yellow chin. In the fanned tail you can see white inner vanes to the outer tail feathers. The illustration shows an adult male, below, and female, above.

Palm Warbler, *Dendroica palmarum*
Family Parulidae (Wood Warblers)
Size: 5.5"
Range: Throughout Florida; winter
Habitat: Thickets near spruce bogs, open grassland

The palm warbler forages on the ground for insects while constantly bobbing its tail. It is brownish above with darker streaking, and pale brown gray below with dark streaking. Its chin and undertail coverts are bright yellow. The head has a dark eye stripe, a pale superciliary stripe, and a dark rufous crown. Nonbreeding adults are paler, with a gray chin and brown crown. Outer tail feathers show small white patches and contrast with an olive-yellow rump. Two races of this species occur in Florida: the "yellow," with a yellow underside, and the "brown," with a pale gray belly and brown streaking. The illustration shows a breeding adult of the "brown" form.

Pine Warbler, *Dendroica pinus*
Family Parulidae (Wood Warblers)
Size: 5.5"
Range: Throughout Florida; year-round
Habitat: Pine and mixed pine woodlands

The pine warbler creeps along pine branches picking insects from the bark. It is a rounded, long-winged warbler with a relatively thick bill. Its plumage is olive green above with gray wings, and yellow below streaked with olive. Its belly and undertail coverts are white. The yellow of the chin extends under the auricular area; a faint "spectacle" is formed by the light lores and eye ring, and there are two clearly marked white wing bars. The female is paler overall, and the juvenile lacks yellow on the chin and underparts. The outer tail feathers show white patches. The illustration shows an adult male.

Prairie Warbler, *Dendroica discolor*
Family Parulidae (Wood Warblers)
Size: 4.5"
Range: Throughout Florida; year-round
Habitat: Mangroves, early succession forests, shrubs

The prairie warbler is small, plump, and long-tailed, with a ris-ing, buzzy song that it sometimes sings from a treetop perch. It is olive green above and bright yellow below, with black streaking along its sides topped by a distinct spot just behind the bottom of the chin. A dark half circle swoops underneath the eye, and sometimes rusty streaking is seen on the bird's mantle. Its outer tail feathers are white. The female is slightly paler overall. Prairie warblers forage through the low branches of the understory for insects and spiders. The illustration shows an adult male.

Prothonotary Warbler, *Protonotaria citrea*
Family Parulidae (Wood Warblers)
Size: 5.5"
Range: Throughout Florida; summer
Habitat: Wooded swamps

Also known as the golden swamp warbler, the prothonotary warbler is fairly large, with a short tail, a relatively large head, and a long, sharp bill. Its head and underparts are a rich yellow to yellow-orange, and the undertail coverts are white. Its wings and tail are blue-gray and there is an olive green mantle. Females and juveniles are paler overall, with an olive cast to the head. Prothonotary warblers forage through the understory for insects. The illustration shows an adult male.

Yellow-throated Warbler, *Dendroica dominica*
Family Parulidae (Wood Warblers)
Size: 5.25"
Range: Throughout Florida; year-round
Habitat: Coniferous and mixed woodlands near water

The yellow-throated warbler is an elongated, long-billed bird that forages high in the tree canopy, picking insects from the bark. Its plumage is slate gray above and white below, heavily streaked with black, and it has a clean yellow chin and breast. There is a bold face pattern, with a white supercilium and lower eye arc bordered by a black eye stripe and auricular area. Behind the ear is a distinctive white patch. The dark back contrasts with two white wing bars. The bird's outer tail feathers show patches of white. The illustration shows an adult male.

Common Yellowthroat, *Geothlypis trichas*
Family Parulidae (Wood Warblers)
Size: 5"
Range: Throughout Florida; year-round
Habitat: Low vegetation near water, swamps, fields

The common yellowthroat scampers through the undergrowth foraging for insects and spiders in a somewhat wrenlike manner. It is a plump, little warbler that often cocks up its tail. Its plumage is olive-brown above, pale brown to whitish below, with bright yellow undertail coverts and breast/chin region. The male has a black facial mask trailed by a fuzzy white area on its nape. Females lack the facial mask. The illustration shows an adult male, below, and female, above.

Eastern Towhee, *Pipilo erythrophthalmus*
Family Emberizidae (Sparrows)
Size: 8"
Range: Throughout Florida; year-round
Habitat: Thickets, suburban shrubs, gardens

The eastern towhee is a large, long-tailed sparrow with a thick, short bill and sturdy legs. It forages on the ground in dense cover by kicking both feet back at once to uncover insects, seeds, and worms. It is black above, including the head and upper breast, and has rufous sides and a white belly. The base of its primaries are white, as are the corners of its tail. Its eye color ranges from red to white, depending on the region. Females are like the males, but are brown above. The towhee song is a musical *drink-your-teee*. The eastern towhee was once conspecific with the spotted towhee as the rufous-sided towhee. The illustration shows an adult male.

Chipping Sparrow, *Spizella passerina*
Family Emberizidae (Sparrows)
Size: 5.5"
Range: Throughout Florida; year-round
Habitat: Dry fields, woodland edges, gardens

The chipping sparrow is a medium-size sparrow with a slightly notched tail and a rounded crest. It is barred black and brown on the upper parts, with a gray rump, and is pale gray below. Its head has a rufous crown, a white superciliary stripe, a dark eye line, and a white throat. Its bill is short, conical, and pointed. The sexes are similar, and in winter the adults are duller and lack the rufous color on their crowns. Chipping sparrows feed from trees or on open ground in loose flocks, searching for seeds and insects. The voice is a rapid, staccato chipping sound. The illustration shows a breeding (summer) adult.

Summer Tanager, *Piranga rubra*
Family Cardinalidae (Tanagers, Grosbeaks, and Buntings)
Size: 7.75"
Range: Throughout Florida; year-round
Habitat: Mixed pine and oak woodlands

The summer tanager lives high in the tree canopy, where it voices a musical song and forages for insects and fruit. It is a relatively large, heavy-billed tanager with a crown that is often peaked in the middle. The male is variable shades of red over the entire body, while the female is olive or brownish yellow above and dull yellow below. Juveniles are similar to the females but have patchy red heads and breasts. The illustration shows an adult male.

Northern Cardinal, *Cardinalis cardinalis*
Family Cardinalidae (Tanagers, Grosbeaks, and Buntings)
Size: 8.5"
Range: Throughout Florida; year-round
Habitat: Woodlands with thickets, suburban gardens

The northern cardinal, with its thick, powerful bill, eats mostly seeds but it will also forage for fruit and insects. The cardinal is often found in pairs and is quite common at suburban feeders. It is a long-tailed songbird with a thick, short, orange bill and a tall crest. The male is red overall, with a black mask and chin. The female is brownish above, dusky below, crested, and has a dark front to her face. Juveniles are similar in color to the female, but have black bills. The voice is a musical *weeta-weeta* or *woit* heard from a tall, exposed perch. The illustration shows an adult male, below, and female, above.

Painted Bunting, *Passerina ciris*
Family Cardinalidae (Tanagers, Grosbeaks, and Buntings)
Size: 5.5"
Range: Throughout Florida; year-round
Habitat: Edges of woodlands, brushy areas, gardens

Like a rainbow on wings, the painted bunting is one of the most colorful birds. It is similar in shape to other buntings, and the plumage is markedly different between the sexes. The male has a green mantle and wings, red-orange to rusty underparts and rump, and a brilliant blue head with a red eye ring. The female is yellowish green above and pale yellow-green below, with a pale eye ring. Often secretive and difficult to find, painted buntings scamper in the understory or on the ground, foraging for insects, seeds, and fruit. However, they may also visit feeders. The illustration shows an adult male, below, and female, above.

Eastern Meadowlark, *Sturnella magna*
Family Icteridae (Blackbirds, Grackles, and Orioles)
Size: 9.5"
Range: Throughout Florida; year-round
Habitat: Open fields, grasslands, meadows

The eastern meadowlark is a chunky, short-tailed icterid with a flat head and a long, pointed bill. It is heavily streaked and barred above, and yellow beneath, with dark streaking. Its head has a dark crown, a white superciliary stripe, a dark eye line, and a yellow chin. On the upper breast is a black, V-shaped necklace that becomes quite pale during the winter months. Meadowlarks gather in loose flocks to pick through grasses for insects and seeds. They often perch on telephone wires or posts to sing their short, whistling phrases. The illustration shows a breeding (summer) adult.

Brown-headed Cowbird, *Molothrus ater*
Family Icteridae (Blackbirds, Grackles, and Orioles)
Size: 7.5"
Range: Throughout Florida; year-round
Habitat: Woodland edges, pastures with livestock, grassy fields

The brown-headed cowbird is a stocky, short-winged, short-tailed blackbird with a short, conical bill. The male is glossy black overall with a chocolate-brown head. The female is light brown overall with faint streaking on the underparts and a pale throat. Cowbirds often feed in flocks with other blackbirds, picking out seeds and insects from the ground. The voice is a number of gurgling, squeaking phrases. Cowbirds practice brood parasitism, whereby they lay their eggs in the nests of other bird species that then raise the cowbird young. Hence, their presence often reduces the populations of other songbirds. The illustration shows an adult male.

Red-winged Blackbird, *Agelaius phoeniceus*
Family Icteridae (Blackbirds, Grackles, and Orioles)
Size: 8.5"
Range: Throughout Florida; year-round
Habitat: Marshes, meadows, agricultural areas near water

The red-winged blackbird is a widespread, ubiquitous, chunky meadow dweller that forms huge flocks during the nonbreeding season. The male is deep black overall, with bright orange-red lesser coverts and pale median coverts that form an obvious shoulder patch in flight but may be partially concealed on the perched bird. The female is barred tan and dark brown overall, with a pale superciliary stripe and malar patch. Red-winged blackbirds forage the marshland for insects, spiders, and seeds. The voice is a loud, raspy, vibrating *konk-a-leee* given from a perch atop a tall reed or branch. The illustration shows an adult male, below, and female, above.

Common Grackle, *Quiscalus quiscula*
Family Icteridae (Blackbirds, Grackles, and Orioles)
Size: 12.5"
Range: Throughout Florida; year-round
Habitat: Pastures, open woodlands, urban parks

The common grackle is a large blackbird, but is smaller than the boat-tailed grackle. Its body is elongated, with a long, heavy bill and a long tail that is fatter toward the tip and is often folded into a keel shape. The grackle's plumage is overall black, with a metallic sheen of purple on the head and brown on the wings and underside. The eyes are a contrasting light yellow color. Quite social, grackles form huge flocks with other blackbirds and forage on the ground for just about any kind of food, including insects, grains, refuse, and crustaceans. The voice is a high-pitched, rasping trill. The illustration shows an adult male.

Baltimore Oriole, *Icterus galbula*
Family Icteridae (Blackbirds, Grackles, and Orioles)
Size: 8.5"
Range: Throughout Florida; winter
Habitat: Deciduous woodlands, suburban gardens, parks

The Baltimore oriole is a somewhat stocky icterid with a short, squared tail and a straight, tapered bill. The male is bright yellow-orange with a black hood. Its wings are black with white edging on the flight feathers and coverts, and yellow-orange shoulder patches. The tail is orange, with black along the base and down the middle. The female is paler along the sides, with a white shoulder patch, a mottled, yellow-and-brown head, and a plain tail. The oriole forages for insects, fruit, and nectar in the leafy canopy. It is sometimes considered, with Bullock's oriole, as one species, the northern oriole. The illustration shows an adult male, below, and female, above.

American Goldfinch, *Spinus tristis*
Family Fringillidae (Finches)
Size: 5"
Range: Throughout Florida; winter
Habitat: Open fields, marshes, urban feeders

The American goldfinch is small, cheerful, and social, with a short, notched tail and a small, conical bill. In winter it is brownish gray, lighter underneath, with black wings and tail. There is bright yellow on the shoulders, around the eyes, and along the chin, and there are two white wing bars. In breeding plumage, the male becomes light yellow across his back, undersides, and head, and develops a black forehead and loral area. Also, his bill becomes orange. Females have similar plumage to the males in winter. Goldfinches forage by actively searching for insects and seeds of all kinds, particularly thistle. The voice is a meandering, musical warble, including high cheep notes. The illustration shows a breeding male, below, and a nonbreeding male, above.

REPTILES

American Alligator, *Alligator mississippiensis*
Family Alligatoridae (Alligators)
Size: Up to 12'; males larger than females
Range: Throughout Florida
Habitat: Most aquatic environments, including fresh or brackish
swamps and mangroves

The American alligator is the largest reptile in North America. Once threatened with extinction, it is now protected and maintaining stable populations. It is strong and compact, with a large, thick head, a rounded snout, short limbs, and imposing, teeth-laden jaws. The skin is lined with ridges along the back and colored gray to greenish above, and paler underneath. Juveniles are black with pale, cream-colored bands. American alligators are adept swimmers, and they move slowly on land except for occasional rapid lunges. Alligators are carnivores and will eat almost any available food, including fish, reptiles, birds, and mammals to the size of livestock.

American Crocodile, *Crocodylus acutus*
Family Crocodylidae (Crocodiles)
Size: Up to 15'
Range: Southern tip of Florida and the Keys
Habitat: Swamps, bogs, mangroves, salt marshes

The American crocodile is an endangered, tropical species that, within North America, is found only in the extreme southern portions of Florida. Its body is very large, with a long tail, thick stubby legs, and a narrow, elongated snout. Its scaled skin has raised ridges on the back and tail. It is colored grayish green with irregular black bands across the body and tail; the bands become less obvious in older individuals. With its mouth closed, the large teeth of the lower jaw are visible, unlike in alligators. American crocodiles feed on fish, birds, amphibians, small mammals, and crabs, and often rest with their mouths held open.

Black Racer, *Coluber constrictor*
Family Colubridae (Colubrid Snakes)
Size: Up to 5'
Range: Throughout Florida
Habitat: Brush and thickets, suburbs; often found near water

One of Florida's more common snakes, the black racer is a long, thin, speedy snake often sighted in residential areas. Its eyes are dark and relatively large, its neck is thin, and its scales are smooth. Its color is black or dark gray above, paler below, with a whitish chin and a brown snout. Young snakes are paler overall, with rounded, brownish spots along the back. Burrowing during the night, black racers are most active in the daytime, foraging on the ground for insects or small vertebrates, and are capable of climbing trees to escape danger. Although not poisonous, they are capable of inflicting a painful bite.

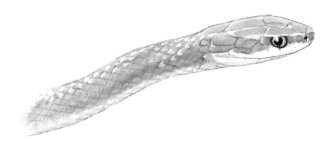

Rough Green Snake, *Opheodrys aestivus*
Family Colubridae (Colubrid Snakes)
Size: Up to 45"
Range: Throughout Florida
Habitat: Brushy areas near water including swamps, as well as in trees and vines

The rough green snake is a lithe and graceful snake that prefers life above ground, slithering though branches and vines. It is narrow with a small head, and has scales with small ridges along their centers (keeled). Adults are well camouflaged in leafy vegetation, being unmarked yellow-green above and on the sides, and white or pale yellow along the belly and lower face. Juveniles are grayish green. Rough green snakes are most active during the day, foraging for insects and spiders, which they swallow whole. They are also good swimmers, and will enter the water to escape danger.

Common Garter Snake, *Thamnophis sirtalis*
Family Colubridae (Colubrid Snakes)
Size: Up to 40"
Range: Throughout Florida
Habitat: Well vegetated areas near water, including marshes, and in
urban parks

The garter snake is widespread and common, with more than ten subspecies. The garter snake commonly frequents developed areas and home gardens. The most common form in Florida is the eastern garter snake, whose body is thin and medium-size, with a head slightly wider than the body and with relatively large eyes. The garter snake's skin has keeled scales, and is quite variable in color, ranging from dark olive-gray to pale orange-brown, and usually showing three pale longitudinal stripes—one running across the top to the back, and two along the sides. Often there are blackish spots between the stripes. The underparts are pale gray. Garter snakes freely move from land to water, and feed on insects, aquatic invertebrates, fish, and small mammals. They are relatively harmless, but can bite and may emit foul-smelling fluid if trapped.

Eastern Coral Snake, *Micrurus fulvius*
Family Elapidae (Cobra-type Snakes)
Size: Up to 24" or longer
Range: Throughout Florida
Habitat: Woodlands near water, rural gardens, hammocks

The eastern coral snake is generally secretive in nature, but caution is advised if one is encountered as its bite is venomous and can be fatal. The coral snake's body is slender, with smooth, shiny scales and a small, blunt-tipped head (the head is no wider than the body). Its color is striking, with wide red and black bands separated by thinner, yellow bands. Its head is black with a wide yellow band just behind the eyes. Many harmless snakes have similar colors, but one distinguishing mark of the coral snake is that the red and yellow bands are always adjacent to one another. Coral snakes move through dense leaf litter and fallen wood, feeding on smaller snakes, other reptiles, and amphibians.

Cottonmouth, *Agkistrodon piscivorus*
Family Viperidae (Vipers)
Size: Up to 6' long
Range: Throughout Florida
Habitat: Swamps, lakes, streams, wetlands

Also known as the water moccasin, the cottonmouth is a mostly aquatic snake that deserves much caution, as its bite can be fatal. It is a large, thick snake, with a head noticeably wider than its body and an abruptly tapering tail. The color is variably blackish to greenish brown, paler below, with younger individuals showing ragged, lighter bands. There is a dark, light-bordered patch behind the eyes, and the inside of the mouth is whitish (thus the common name). A member of the pit viper family, it has heat-sensing pits between the eyes and nostrils. Mostly nocturnal, cottonmouths feed on fish, amphibians, birds, and other snakes, and they usually swim with their heads well out of the water.

Green Sea Turtle, *Chelonia mydas*
Family Cheloniidae (Sea Turtles)
Size: Up to 4' (shell)
Range: Most of coastal Florida, especially the eastern coast
Habitat: Shallow to deep marine waters; on beaches when laying eggs

Also known as the green turtle, this is medium-size sea turtle has a broad, oval, smooth shell and elongate limbs flattened into powerful flippers. The upper shell (carapace) is brownish to olive green with variable, radiating striations, while the lower shell (plastron) is pale tan to whitish. The common name refers to the greenish color of its fat. Green turtles feed underwater on marine plants, but must surface to breathe. The young hatch on their own, and live in the open ocean for a year before returning to coastal waters. These turtles are threatened, their status partly due to the destruction of nesting sites and entanglement in fishing nets.

Gopher Tortoise, *Gopherus polyphemus*
Family Testudinidae (Tortoises)
Size: Up to 13" (shell)
Range: Most of Florida except the Keys
Habitat: Sandy soils of open woodlands, scrubby grasslands, coastal dunes

The gopher tortoise is terrestrial, with a tall, domed upper shell
(carapace) that has concentric ridges and grooves within the
individual shell segments. Its head is short-necked, rounded, and
thick; the front legs are flattened, with heavy scales and claws,
while the rear legs are short and stumpy. The carapace is brownish, the lower shell (plastron) is yellowish, and the body parts are
gray-brown. Gopher tortoises dig long burrows underground for
shelter, and in turn provide homes for many other animals, including burrowing owls, rodents, and snakes. They feed during the
day on plants, and as a defense can retract their heads and legs
completely into their shells.

Florida Red-bellied Turtle, *Pseudemys nelson*
Family Emydidae (Pond Turtles)
Size: Up to 12" (shell)
Range: Central and southern Florida
Habitat: Stagnant fresh or brackish waters; ponds, swamps, mangroves

Found only in Florida and southern Georgia, the Florida red-bellied turtle is a large pond turtle with a thick, high-domed shell. Its feet have webbed toes for swimming, with longer claws on the front feet. Its upper jaw has two toothlike projections (only noticeable at close range). The upper shell (carapace) is blackish with rusty red markings, the lower shell (plastron) is yellowish orange, and the body parts are black with yellow stripes. Florida red-bellied turtles spend much time basking on rocks or logs in the water, and feed on aquatic plants.

Snapping Turtle, *Chelydra serpentina*
Family Chelydridae (Snapping Turtles)
Size: Up to 14" (shell)
Range: Northern Florida and the Panhandle region
Habitat: Most freshwater environments, especially those with plentiful water plants

The snapping turtle is large and stocky, with a relatively small shell for its body size, a long tapered tail, and a massive head with powerful jaws. Its color is variable, but usually is some shade of brown, often obscured by a coating of algae. The feet are strong with long claws. Snapping turtles may rest underwater on muddy bottoms or bask on rocks in the sun to warm themselves. They forage for a wide variety of prey, including plants, insects, aquatic invertebrates, small mammals, amphibians, or birds. Use caution around this turtle, as it can give a painful bite.

Eastern Fence Lizard, *Sceloporus undulatus*
Family Phrynosomatidae (Fence and Horned Lizards)
Size: Up to 6", including tail
Range: Central and northern Florida
Habitat: A wide variety of sunny habitats, including grasslands, woodlands, and brushy areas

The eastern fence lizard includes several subspecies of varying color patterns, including grayish or brownish with longitudinal striping, spotting, or a combination thereof. In Florida, most individuals have dark, ragged bars across the back, and males show blue patches on the belly and chin. It is a compact, long-tailed lizard with big feet, a blunt face, and scaled, dry skin. Solitary and active during the day, fence lizards scurry through sheltered areas or among trees, and feed on all kinds of insects and other invertebrates.

Green Anole, *Anolis carolinensis*
Family Polychrotidae (Anoles)
Size: Up to 8", including tail
Range: Throughout Florida
Habitat: Virtually any environment with trees, vines, and tall brush, including buildings and fences in urban areas

The green anole is a common arboreal lizard that is often raised as a pet. It has a thin body, a long tail, a pointed snout, and padded toes to aid in climbing on vertical surfaces. Its color can vary from bright green to brown or gray, depending on environmental factors or stress, but the underside is always paler. Males develop an extendible, pinkish skin flap under the throat (the "throat fan"). Active during the day, green anoles often bask head down on tree branches, buildings, or fences. They forage with stealth and patience for prey of insects or other invertebrates.

Mediterranean Gecko, *Hemidactylus turcicus*
Family Gekkonidae (Geckos)
Size: Up to 5", including tail
Range: Throughout Florida
Habitat: Developed areas, walls of buildings, trees, lights at night

The Mediterranean gecko is native to the Mediterranean region and has been introduced to the southern United States, where it maintains a stable or growing population. It has a large head with a rounded snout, eyes that are lidless and have vertical pupils, and feet with adhesive pads to aid in climbing vertical surfaces. The skin color can range from pale gray to brownish or tan with dark spots (colors are usually palest at night). The gecko's body is covered with rough, whitish bumps. Most active at night, Mediterranean geckos feed on moths and other insects by waiting quietly, then snatching up prey as it draws near. They make a high-pitched squeak or chirp, somewhat like a mouse or a small bird.

AMPHIBIANS

Bullfrog, *Rana catesbeiana*
Family Ranidae (True Frogs)
Size: Up to 6"
Range: Throughout Florida except for the Keys
Habitat: Ponds and lakes with dense vegetation

North America's largest frog, the bullfrog is squat and heavy-bodied, with massive rear legs allowing for quick, strong leaps and swift swimming. Its smooth skin is green to brownish green, with brown or gray mottling or spotting, and a pale belly. It has large, external eardrums just behind its eyes. Bullfrogs are mostly nocturnal and always found in or near a body of water. Their large mouths enable them to feed on a wide variety of prey, including insects, aquatic invertebrates, and even small mammals or birds.

Southern Leopard Frog, *Lithobates sphenocephalus*
Family Ranidae (True Frogs)
Size: Up to 4"
Range: Throughout Florida
Habitat: Freshwater or brackish marshes, streams, ponds, moist fields

The southern leopard frog is squat and bony, with narrow hind-quarters and long, powerful rear legs for leaping. There are two pale, narrow ridges of skin along either side of the frog's back. Leopard frogs also have a light stripe above the mouth, and the eardrums usually have a light-colored central spot. The overall color of its smooth skin is green to brownish, with large, dark spots bordered by a lighter color, giving the frog its common name. Leopard frogs skulk in water or vegetation, foraging for insects and invertebrates. Their large mouths allow them to eat fairly large prey, including small birds or other frogs.

Southern Toad, *Anaxyrus terrestris*
Family Bufonidae (Toads)
Size: Up to 3.5"
Range: Throughout Florida
Habitat: Sandy pine-oak woodlands, marshes, rural gardens

The southern toad is a medium-size, stocky toad with conspicuous protuberances behind the eyes, and enlarged, oval, raised lumps (parotid glands) behind the eardrums. The skin is dry, covered with warts, variably brown, gray, or nearly black with dark spotting above, and paler on the belly (males have a dark throat). Often there is a thin, pale dorsal stripe running the length of the back. Southern toads keep to burrows during the day, emerging at night to feed on insects and other invertebrates. They have an alarming, high-pitched, trilled voice.

Peninsula Newt, *Notophthalmus viridescens*
Family Salamandridae (Newts)
Size: Up to 3.5"
Range: Throughout Florida except for the Keys
Habitat: Wetlands, ponds, and nearby meadows or woodlands

Newts are elongate, short-legged, long-tailed, semiaquatic rela-
tives of salamanders with rough-textured (not slimy) skin. They
are born in the water, mature on land, then return to the water
at adulthood. The peninsula newt has coloration that varies from
orange in the immature stage to greenish brown to blackish in
the adult, with a dark orange belly and numerous tiny black spots
overall. Newts are adept swimmers, propelled by undulating their
bodies and long, flattened tails. They forage day or night in the
water or on the ground for insects, larvae, fish or frog eggs, and
worms. They may burrow or remain active in the water during
winter months.

FISH

Tiger Shark, *Galeocerdo cuvier*
Family Carcharhinidae (Requiem Sharks)
Size: 8–15'
Range: Coastal Florida
Habitat: Open ocean, into channels and bays

The formidable tiger shark is one of the world's largest sharks, and is widespread throughout tropical waters. It has a blunt snout, sharp teeth, a triangular dorsal fin, narrow pectoral fins, and an asymmetrical tail with an elongated upper lobe. The body is blue-gray to brown-gray above and paler below. Younger individuals also have dark spotting and vertical stripes along the sides, which fade in maturity. Mostly solitary, tiger sharks continuously cruise in search of prey, which they locate using an acute sense of smell and electrical sensors. They are known to attack humans, and indiscriminately feed on anything they find, including fish, squid, turtles, and seals.

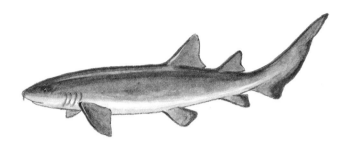

Nurse Shark, *Ginglymostoma cirratum*
Family Ginglymostomatidae (Nurse Sharks)
Size: Up to 14'
Range: Coastal Florida
Habitat: Shallow to moderately deep ocean, coral reefs, channels

The nurse shark is large, slow-moving, and common to shallow, near-shore waters. It is relatively big-headed, with large pectoral fins and a highly asymmetrical tail with an elongated top lobe and a diminutive bottom lobe. Its color is brownish above and whitish or tawny below. The front of the snout bears two fleshy appendages (barbels) as sensing organs. During the day, the nurse shark rests in groups in protected areas, becoming active at night to search for a wide variety of prey including fish, squid, crustaceans, and even corals, which it crunches with its strong jaws and teeth.

Spotted Eagle Ray, *Aetobatus narinari*
Family Myliobatidae (Eagle Rays)
Size: ~4' body; tail to 10'
Range: Coastal Florida
Habitat: Coastal bays, estuaries, shallow near-shore waters

The spotted eagle ray is a beautiful, graceful fish, related to sharks, that uses its broad pectoral fins in a birdlike manner to glide through the water. The body is flattened overall, with a short head, a small dorsal fin, and an extremely long, thin tail that bears sharp, poisonous barbs. It is sometimes called the "duck-billed ray" because its snout resembles the flat bill of a duck. Its color is blackish with small white spots above, and uniformly white below. Spotted eagle rays feed on bottom-dwelling crustaceans and mollusks, which they can crush with their strong jaws and teeth.

Largemouth Bass, *Micropterus salmoides*
Family Centrarchidae (Sunfish)
Size: Up to 29"
Range: Throughout Florida
Habitat: Shallow freshwater lakes, rivers, and ponds

The state freshwater fish of Florida, the largemouth bass is a favorite of anglers for its tenacious fight when hooked. It is an elongate member of the sunfish family, with a mouth that extends to the rear of the eye, two separate dorsal fins (the first spiny and the second soft), and an indented tail fin. Its color is greenish gray above, with a blotchy, blackish lateral stripe (fading with age), and a whitish belly. Largemouth bass skulk through warmer and weedier parts of creeks or lakes foraging for a wide variety of aquatic prey, including crustaceans, insects, other fish, and frogs.

Bluegill, *Lepomis macrochirus*
Family Centrarchidae (Sunfish)
Size: Up to 10"
Range: Throughout Florida
Habitat: Shallow lakes and rivers with aquatic plants

Also known as the "bream," the bluegill is a popular freshwater sport fish. It has an oval, highly compressed body with a small mouth, a dorsal fin that is elongated to the rear, and a slightly forked tail fin. Its color is grayish green above, with indistinct, darker, broad vertical bars along the sides, and a dark blue-black patch on the operculum. The underparts are silvery to yellow, becoming red-orange on the chest of the spawning male. Blue-gill feed on insects, insect larvae, crustaceans, and small fish. The male is illustrated.

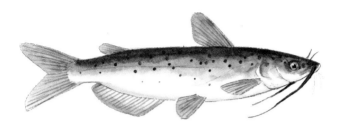

Channel Catfish, *Ictalurus punctatus*
Family Ictaluridae (Catfish)
Size: Up to 40"
Range: Throughout Florida except in the far south
Habitat: Freshwater lakes and streams

The channel catfish is common, widespread, and popular as a sport fish. Its body is elongate and narrow, with a long head, a deeply forked tail fin, a tall, pointed dorsal fin, a long anal fin, and a small adipose fin. It has three sets of sensory barbels: a long black pair that originates above the mouth, a group of white ones growing from its chin, and two short black ones on its forehead. Its color is bluish gray above, whitish below, with sparse black spots along the sides. Channel catfish are most active at night, when they forage on the bottom of lakes and streams for a variety of prey including mollusks, worms, and insect larvae, but they may also feed for smaller fish in open water.

Florida Gar, *Lepisosteus platyrhincus*
Family Lepisosteidae (Gars)
Size: Up to 30"
Range: Throughout the Florida peninsula
Habitat: Vegetated rivers, lakes, estuaries, saltwater channels, swamps

The Florida gar is an ancient species of fish, able to survive in either fresh or brackish waters using its gills and an air bladder to acquire oxygen. The body is rounded and highly elongated, with a long, thin snout equipped with sharp teeth. Its dorsal fin is tall and set far to the rear, and its tail fin is rounded. The skin is composed of large, tough scales that are brownish green above and whitish below, with dark spotting on the sides. Florida gars feed on a variety of fish and aquatic invertebrates, and can often be seen floating at the surface of the water.

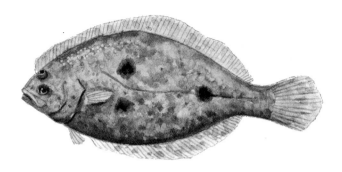

Gulf Flounder, *Paralichthys albigutta*
Family Paralichthyidae (Left-Eye Flounder)
Size: Up to 15"
Range: Coastal Florida
Habitat: Shallow coastal waters with sand or mud bottoms

Flounders are curious fish that are extremely flattened and have both eyes on one side of the head, an adaptation to a lifestyle of lying flat on the ocean floor. The gulf flounder is oval, with a small head and a broad, wedge-shaped tail fin. Its color is mottled in brown tones, and varies depending upon the color of the sub-strate. It also has three distinct, black spots on the upper side. Gulf flounders nestle cryptically in sand or mud and swiftly snatch prey with their sharp teeth. They are a popular sport fish in Florida.

Black Sea Bass, *Centropristis striata*
Family Serranidae (Groupers)
Size: Up to 24"
Range: Coastal Florida
Habitat: Shallow coastal waters with rocky bottoms

The black sea bass is a stout, tall-backed member of the grouper family and an important game fish. It has high-set eyes, a dorsal fin with spines on the front half, fleshy rays on the back half, and a rounded tail fin that, in mature fish, has a thin, longer extension on the top or bottom edge. Its color is gray to gray-brown on the back, paler on the sides and bottom, with variable dark bands along the sides and white spotting on the dorsal fin. The dark markings fade upon removal from water. Black sea bass feed on bottom-dwelling crustaceans and invertebrates, and often congregate at jetties and wrecks.

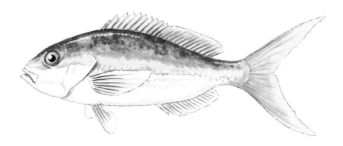

Yellowtail Snapper, *Ocyurus chrysurus*
Family Lutjanidae (Snappers)
Size: Up to 24"
Range: Coastal Florida
Habitat: Coastal waters, usually over coral reefs

The lovely yellowtail snapper is an important game fish and is also popular with divers. It is stout, with large eyes, a relatively small mouth, a forked tail tin, and a long, continuous dorsal fin. Its color is silvery blue-gray above and whitish below, with a striking, golden yellow stripe along the sides, on the tail, and on the dorsal fin. Yellowtail snappers form sparse schools, feeding near the bottom or in open waters around coral reefs for crustaceans and small fish. Younger fish may seek shelter in marine algae.

Tarpon, *Megalops atlanticus*
Family Megalopidae (Tarpons)
Size: Up to 8'
Range: Coastal Florida; more common in the south
Habitat: Offshore to inshore coastal waters, estuaries, canals

The tarpon is a very large, popular sport fish and a strong, fast swimmer. Its body is elongate and compressed. Its short, triangular dorsal fin has a long filament on the back end. Its tail fin is strongly forked, and its mouth has a protruding lower mandible. Its color is blue-gray above and silvery on the sides and belly. It has large, smooth scales and dark gray fins. Younger tarpons may be found in brackish, estuarine water, while adults prefer to stay offshore. Tarpons are mostly active at night, feeding on crustaceans and fish.

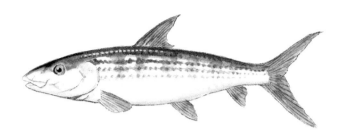

Bonefish, *Albula vulpes*
Family Albulidae (Bonefish)
Size: Up to 36"
Range: Coastal Florida
Habitat: Shallow offshore waters; especially near mangroves and muddy bottoms

The bonefish is a popular sport fish, and a strong, swift swimmer in shallow waters. Its body is elongate, somewhat compressed, with a single, triangular dorsal fin, a strongly forked tail fin, a projecting, conical snout, and a lower mandible that is shorter than the upper mandible. Its color is overall silvery gray, with darker lateral stripes and faint barring along the sides, and dark fins that are sometimes yellowish at their bases. Bonefish move landward with the rising tide to feed on small marine prey such as crustaceans, mollusks, and worms, often upending in the shallows to reveal their tail fins.

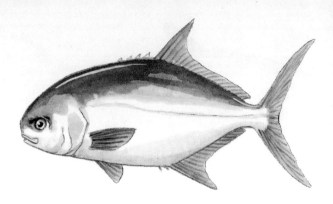

Florida Pompano, *Trachinotus carolinus*
Family Carangidae (Jacks)
Size: Up to 16"
Range: Coastal Florida
Habitat: Shallow near-shore coastal waters, including inlets, surf zones

The Florida pompano is a popular sport and commercial fish that may sometimes be seen jumping out of the water in the surf. It has a laterally compressed oval body, a rounded forehead, and a blunt snout. The caudal peduncle is very narrow, rising to a tall and forked tail fin. The dorsal and anal fins are nearly symmetrical; pointed then tapering, and long. The pompano's color is blue to green-gray above, silver along the sides, and white to yellow below. Florida pompanos forage in sandy and muddy bottoms for mollusks and crustaceans. They may move offshore to deeper water in the winter.

Great Barracuda, *Sphyraena barracuda*
Family Sphyraenidae (Barracudas)
Size: Up to 6'
Range: Coastal Florida
Habitat: Open seas, waters with sandy or muddy bottoms, mangroves

The barracuda is a fearsome-looking tropical fish that is ruthless with its prey but generally uninterested in attacking humans, although caution is advised and bites have been reported. It has a large, elongate body with a roundish cross-section, and a pointed, tooth-laden mouth with a protruding lower jaw. There are two separate pointed dorsal fins, mirrored below by pelvic and anal fins, and a large, forked tail fin. The barracuda's color is blue-gray above and silvery white on the sides and bottom, with sparse black spots on the sides. The young may form groups, but adult barracudas are generally solitary. They prey on fish by ambush, lurking and moving slowly before suddenly chasing prey with fast, direct swimming.

Blue Marlin, *Makaira nigricans*
Family Istiophoridae (Billfish)
Size: Up to 10' or longer
Range: Coastal Florida
Habitat: Offshore waters, generally near the surface

The blue marlin is a huge, streamlined, extremely fast fish, highly prized by sport fishermen. It has a steep forehead and a thick body up front that gradually tapers to a narrow peduncle and tall, thin, curving tail fin. Perhaps most striking is the elongated, spearlike snout that overlaps the much shorter lower mandible. The dorsal fin is tall in front, quickly tapering to a narrow strip that extends along most of the back. Its color is deep blue to brownish above, white below, with pale blue barring on the sides. The abundance of blue marlins varies as they migrate according to the seasons.

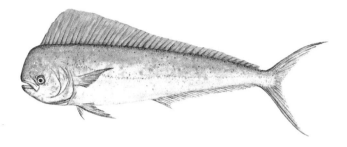

Dolphinfish, *Coryphaena hippurus*
Family Coryphaenidae (Dolphinfish)
Size: Up to 50"
Range: Coastal Florida
Habitat: Offshore waters, generally near the surface

Also known as the dorado, or simply as the dolphin, the dolphin-fish is a large, marine sport fish renowned for its fast swimming speed and great strength. Its body is long and compressed, with a tall forehead (highest in males). A long dorsal fin runs the length of the back; the dolphinfish also has a long anal fin and a deeply forked tail fin that arises from a narrow peduncle (base of the tail). The color is striking, with hues of brilliant yellow or bluish green along the back, dorsal fin, and upper sides, silver or gold along the sides and bottom, and small blue spots throughout. These colors quickly fade upon death. Dolphinfish chase flying fish close to the surface, or congregate in beds of algae, feeding on smaller fish, shrimp, and crustaceans.

BUTTERFLIES

Giant Swallowtail, *Papilio cresphontes*
Family Papilionidae (Swallowtails and Parnassians)
Size: Wingspan 4–6"
Range: Throughout Florida
Habitat: Orchards, gardens

The giant swallowtail is the largest butterfly in North America, with a very wide wingspan, scalloped hind wings, and long, bulbous tail projections. The upper-side wings are dark brown to black overall, with a wide yellow band traversing the entire length, and large, yellow submarginal spots across the hind wings and lower forewings. The tails have a distinct yellow spot, and hind wings show orange and blue anal spots. The underside is pale yellow, with dark markings along cell borders and blue crescents on the hind wing. The caterpillar is smooth, mottled brown and white, and has orange, forked horns that release a foul scent. Giant swallowtails fly high, with slow speeds and long glides. The caterpillar eats the leaves of citrus trees (where it is often considered a pest), prickly ash, and hop trees. Adults feed on flower nectar and the salts and moisture from puddles.

Eastern Tiger Swallowtail, *Papilio glaucus*
Family Papilionidae (Swallowtails and Parnassians)
Size: Wingspan 3–5.5"
Range: Throughout Florida
Habitat: Gardens, parks, riversides, forest clearings

Among the largest of North American butterflies, the eastern tiger swallowtail is common throughout its range, is diurnal, and—typical of this family—has distinct projections or "tails" on the hind wings. When alighted and/or feeding, the wings may tremble. Both sexes are bright yellow above, and show ragged black stripes, like those of a tiger, along the anterior forewings. There is black marginal patterning on both fore- and hind wings. The first submarginal spot on the hind wing is orange. The underside is patterned similarly, but is much paler yellow. Females show bright blue posterior markings and, in some southern individuals, may be nearly black overall (looking similar to the spicebush swallowtail). Like the wings, the body also has black and yellow stripes. The caterpillar eats the leaves of trees, including those of the rose, magnolia, laurel and willow families. Adults feed on flower nectar and the salts and moisture from puddles. The caterpillar is brown to greenish, smooth, and plump. The adult female is illustrated.

Falcate Orangetip, *Anthocharis midea*
Family Pieridae (Sulfurs and Whites)
Size: Wingspan 1.5–1.75"
Range: Panhandle region
Habitat: Moist woodlands, stream sides, open fields

The falcate orangetip is a small, white butterfly with a distinctive hooked (falcated) margin to the outer forewing, and lazy, low-to-the-ground flight. The upper-side wings of both sexes are white overall, with a black spot in the discal forewing cell and black marks at the apical margins. The male has solid orange apical regions; this color is absent in females. The undersides of the hind wings are extensively marbled with dark, yellowish green. The body is mottled black and light gray. The butterfly has pale, thin, club-tipped antennae. The caterpillar eats cress and other plants of the mustard family (Brassicaceae), choosing buds, flowers, and seedpods rather than leaves. Adults feed on flower nectar. The caterpillar is green with fine, black, warty spots and two prominent white medial stripes. The illustration is of the adult male.

Southern Dogface, *Zerene cesonia*
Family Pieridae (Sulfurs and Whites)
Size: Wingspan 2–3"
Range: Central and northern Florida
Habitat: Dry fields, open woodlands, farmlands

The southern dogface is a striking sulfur butterfly with rapid flight,
pointed wingtips, and straight outer margins to the forewings. The
male is yellow overall, with broad, black patches at the bases and
outer margins of its forewings, which also show black discal spots.
These markings together give the crude appearance of the head of
a poodlelike dog. The hind wing has a black outer marginal band
with two faint, white, orange-bordered spots near the center. The
female is a plain, dull yellow with black forewing spots, and may
show pinkish patterning on the underside of her hind wings. The
body is mottled yellow and black, darker above than below, and
the butterfly has thin, club-tipped antennae. The caterpillar eats
clover, false indigo, and other plants of the pea family (Fabaceae).
Adults feed on flower nectar. The caterpillar is smooth, green, and
variably marked with yellow and black rings and/or whitish, longitudinal stripes down each side, with an overall covering of small,
blackish warts. The illustration shows the adult male.

Eastern Tailed Blue, *Cupido comyntas*

Family Lycaenidae (Blues, Coppers, Hairstreaks, Gossamer-Wings)
Size: Wingspan 0.75–1.1"
Range: Northern Florida
Habitat: Open fields, roadsides, meadows, disturbed areas

The eastern tailed blue, along with the western tailed blue, is the only butterfly in the group known as "blues" to have tails. The wings of the male are bright violet blue on the upper sides, with white-fringed edges and thick, black, submarginal bands. Above the short, wispy tail on the hind wings are a pair of orange, crescent-shaped spots. The upper side of the female varies from dull gray to dark brown overall, with similar orange markings on the hind wings. In both sexes, the underside is pale gray to brownish, with many black, white-bordered spots. The body is hairy, dark bluish gray to brown above and paler below. The butterfly has thin, black-and-white club-tipped antennae. The caterpillar eats the leaves of plants in the pea family (Fabaceae), including clover, alfalfa, and false indigo. Adults feed on flower nectar and minerals from puddles. The caterpillar is green and finely hairy, with pale lateral stripes and a dark stripe down the back. It secretes honeydew and is often accompanied by ants. The illustration shows the adult male.

Monarch, *Danaus plexippus*
Family Nymphalidae (Brush-Footed Butterflies; Milkweed Butterflies Group)
Size: Wingspan 3–4.5"
Range: Throughout Florida
Habitat: Sunny, open fields, as well as meadows and gardens. During migration, monarchs can be found in almost any environment.

The monarch is a large, sturdy, long-lived butterfly most well known for one of the most incredible migratory journeys of the animal kingdom—its yearly flight to Mexico, where millions of this species gather in discrete, isolated locations. The upper sides of the wings are deep orange, with wide black stripes along the veins and black margins infused with a double row of white spots. Males have narrower black vein markings than females, as well as a small, dark "sex spot" near the base of each hind wing. The underside is marked as above, but the orange is paler. The body is black with white spots on the head and thorax; the monarch has thin, club-tipped antennae. The caterpillar eats the leaves and flowers of milkweed. Adults feed on flower nectar. Both store toxins from milkweed that make them distasteful to predators. The caterpillar is fat, smooth, ringed with black, white, and yellow bands, and has black tentacles behind its head. The adult male is shown.

Red-spotted Purple, *Limenitis arthemis*
Family Nymphalidae (Brush-Footed Butterflies; Admirals and Sisters Group)
Size: Wingspan 2.5–3.75"
Range: Northern and central Florida
Habitat: Deciduous woodlands

The red-spotted purple is the same species as the white admiral, which has a very different color pattern and ranges farther north, although the two may hybridize to create intermediate forms where their ranges overlap. The red-spotted purple superficially resembles the pipevine swallowtail, but lacks the tails. The upper-side wings are dark blue to black, fading to iridescent blue or blue-green near the margins and over most of the hind wing. There are reddish spots along the apex of the forewing. The underside is blu-ish to brown, with several black-bordered orange spots. The body is a dark blue-gray marked with white underneath. The caterpillar eats the leaves of a variety of trees, including wild cherry, willow, poplar, oak, and hawthorn. Adults feed on rotting fruit, dung, and moist soils. The caterpillar, like that of the viceroy, is often said to resemble a bird dropping: It is cream-colored and mottled with dull brown or gray, lumpy, and has two thick tentacles.

Buckeye, *Junonia coenia*
Family Nymphalidae (Brush-Footed Butterflies)
Size: Wingspan 1.75–2.5"
Range: Throughout Florida
Habitat: Open fields, meadows, coastal shorelines

The buckeye is a common medium-size butterfly with pronounced eyespots, which are thought to confuse and deter predators. It tends to remain on or near the ground or low parts of vegetation. The upper-side wings are variable shades of brown, with each wing showing one large and one small multicolored spot. There is also a creamy bar near the apex of the forewing, two orange marks in the discal cell, and scalloped patterning along the entire wing edge. The underside is paler, sometimes achieving a rose cast, with the eyespots still visible. The body is tan to dark brown; it has with pale, club-tipped antennae. The caterpillar eats the leaves, buds, and fruit of plantains, gerardias, and snapdragons. Adults feed on flower nectar and moisture from mud and sand. The caterpillar is mottled black, white, and brown, with dark stripes above, and is covered in black, branched spines.

Malachite, *Siproeta stelenes*
Family Nymphalidae (Brush-Footed Butterflies)
Size: Wingspan 2.5–3.5"
Range: Southern Florida
Habitat: Open woodlands, citrus and avocado orchards, gardens, stream sides

Named for the rare green mineral, the malachite is a beautiful, large butterfly from South and Central America with scalloped wing margins and a short, broad tail on the hind wing. The upper sides of the wings are black, with translucent, pale green marks in a broad band along their interiors and spotting along the inner margins. On the underside the green patterning is similar, but the black is replaced by reddish orange and white. The body is black above and white with oblique dark stripes below. The malachite has thin, club-tipped antennae. The caterpillar eats plants of the Acanthaceae family, including ruellia and blechum. Adults feed on flower nectar, rotting fruit, tree sap, and carrion. The caterpillar is black with rows of branched spines with orange bases, and two long "antlers" at the head.

Gulf Fritillary, *Agraulis vanillae*
Family Nymphalidae (Brush-Footed Butterflies; Heliconians Group)
Size: Wingspan 2.5–3"
Range: Throughout Florida
Habitat: Open fields, forest clearings, gardens

The gulf fritillary is a medium-to-large butterfly with relatively long, narrow forewings that have concave margins. It is more closely related to the longwings or heliconians than to the true fritillaries. The upper sides of its wings are deep orange, with numerous black or dark brown spots and marks; in the central disk of the forewing these encase small white spots. The underside is pale brown, orange at the base of the forewing, and both wings are covered with elongated, silvery white spots, giving the butterfly the alternate name of silver-spotted flambeau. The female is typically darker, with more extensive dark spots. The body is brownish orange above and whitish with dark oblique stripes below. The fritillary has thin, black-and-white banded, club-tipped antennae. The caterpillar eats the leaves of passion vines and passionflowers. Adults feed on flower nectar. The caterpillar is striped brown and orange, and has several rows of long, black, branching spines.

Zebra Longwing, *Heliconius charithonia*

Family Nymphalidae (Brush-Footed Butterflies; Heliconians Group)
Size: Wingspan 2.75–3.5"
Range: Most of Florida except for the Panhandle
Habitat: Moist, open woodlands and disturbed areas

The zebra longwing, also known as the zebra heliconian, or simply the zebra, is an unmistakable member of the subtropical group called heliconians, with a wing shape that is much wider than tall. It is a slow-flying, long-lived butterfly (up to three months) that can be found roosting communally at night. The upper-side wings are boldly patterned with yellow "zebra" stripes set against a jet black background, and also show a row of yellow spots along the lower edges of the hind wings. The underside is similar, but with paler yellow stripes and red spots at the base of the hind wing. The body has a thin abdomen, which is striped black and pale yellow along its length, and the head has large eyes and thin, club-tipped antennae. The caterpillar eats the leaves of passion vines. Adults feed on flower nectar and pollen. The caterpillar is white with small black spots and long, black, hairlike projections.

Long-tailed Skipper, *Urbanus proteus*
Family Hesperiidae (Skippers)
Size: Wingspan 1.75–2.25"
Range: Throughout Florida
Habitat: Most open habitats, gardens, fields

The long-tailed skipper is a colorful member of the group known as skippers, so called because their rapid, darting flight resembles skipping. It has a thick, robust body and relatively short wings, except for the long, broad tails at the bottoms of the hind wings. The upper-side wings are dark brown to black, with scattered white spots on the forewings and the margins of both wings. Both wings also have iridescent blue-green scales at their bases. The underside is brownish overall, with the same white spots on the forewings. The body is iridescent blue and green, with mottled drab earth tones below. The eyes are large, and the antennae are set far apart on the head and end with a hooked tip. The caterpillar eats a variety of plants in the pea family (Fabaceae). Adults feed on flower nectar. The caterpillar is green with tiny yellow spots and a pair of longitudinal yellow stripes, a small, dark brown head, and a constricted neck region. It is sometimes called the "bean leaf roller" because of its habit of hiding in and feeding on leaves it has rolled up. It can be a pest to bean crops.

MOTHS

Rosy Maple Moth, *Dryocampa rubicunda*
Family Saturniidae (Giant Silk Moths)
Size: Wingspan 1.25–2"
Range: Throughout Florida
Habitat: Deciduous woodlands

The rosy maple moth is medium-size, with a stocky, thick body. The upper-side wings are simply patterned, pink at the bases and margins, and pale to bright yellow in between. The underside is patterned similarly but is paler overall. This moth usually holds its wings flat or arched up across its back like a tent. The hairy body is yellow above with pink patches below, and is especially thick at the thorax; the moth has pink legs and broad, orange, feathered antennae. The caterpillar eats leaves from a variety of broadleaf trees, including maple, oak, and beech. Adults do not feed. The light green caterpillar has tiny black dots, an orange-red head, and two black tubercles on the front end.

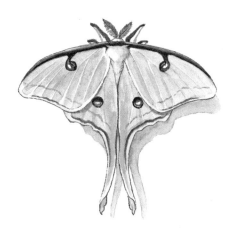

Luna Moth, *Actius luna*
Family Saturniidae (Giant Silk Moths)
Size: Wingspan 3–4.25"
Range: Throughout Florida
Habitat: Deciduous woodlands

The luna moth is very large and striking, with a long, curved tail on each hind wing. The upper-side wings are pale yellowish or bluish green, with a thin brown stripe across the entire leading edge and one distinct eyespot on each wing (the forewing spots are continuous with the stripe of the leading edge). The spots resemble moons, giving the moth its common name. In regions where there are two broods in a year, the moths of the spring brood have thin, reddish outer margins, while those of the fall brood have yellow margins. The body is short and fat, is covered in whitish hairs, and has a dark band across the head, dark legs, and feathered antennae. The sexes are similar, but males have wider feathering on the antennae. The caterpillar eats leaves from a variety of broadleaf trees, including oak, walnut, sweet gum, alder, and birch. Adults do not feed. The caterpillar is plump, light green, and has a yellow stripe across the sides and several rows of dark spots bearing very fine hairs.

Regal Moth, *Citheronia regalis*
Family Saturniidae (Giant Silk Moths)
Size: Wingspan 3.5–6"
Range: Throughout Florida
Habitat: Deciduous woodlands, gardens, parks

The regal moth, also known as the royal walnut moth, is massive and large-bodied. The upper-side wings have a gray-to-brown background color with scattered, pale yellow spots on the inner portion; the margins are unmarked. The hind wing is paler and more orange, while the forewing has unusual red-orange veins. Females are larger than males. The body is thick, well-furred, striped reddish and pale yellow on the thorax and banded on the abdomen. The legs are red-orange, and the antennae are relatively small and feathery. The caterpillar eats leaves from a variety of trees from the walnut family (Juglandaceae), including pecan, as well as hickory and sweet gum. Adults do not feed. The caterpillar, known as the hickory horned devil, is very large and imposing. It is green, marked with black spots and lines, and has several long, arching, red-orange horns on the head and thorax.

Io Moth, *Automeris io*
Family Saturniidae (Giant Silk Moths)
Size: Wingspan 2–3.25"
Range: Throughout Florida
Habitat: Deciduous woodlands, parks, gardens

The Io moth is a medium-to-large silk moth named after a mythical Greek maiden, or perhaps a moon of Jupiter. It is also known as the bull's eye moth because of its large, circular eyespots. Males and females exhibit very different coloration. In the female, the forewings are reddish brown to purplish, with indistinct, paler scalloping and darker marks; when lifted forward they reveal a hind wing with an alarming, large, black eyespot set against a bright yellow background. Males have yellow forewings marked with brown, with a similar eyespot on the hind wing and a patch of red-orange at the base that merges with a red submarginal band. The body is plump and heavily furred, yellow in males, reddish brown in females. The antennae of the males are more heavily feathered. The caterpillar eats a wide variety of plants, including corn, roses, clover, maple, and birch. Adults do not feed. The caterpillar is light green with a red-and-white stripe along each side, and is covered in well-branched, greenish yellow stinging spines. The male is illustrated.

White-lined Sphinx, *Hyles lineata*
Family Sphingidae (Sphinx and Hawk Moths)
Size: Wingspan 2.5–3.5"
Range: Throughout Florida
Habitat: A variety of environments including fields, gardens, and dry scrub

The white-lined sphinx, worldwide in distribution, is sometimes referred to as the striped morning sphinx because it flies during the day as well as night. It is large-bodied, with a tapered abdomen and pointed, narrow wings. The upper side of the forewing is tan and dark brown, with a broad pale stripe from the wing base to tip, crossed by broad, white veins. The hind wing is mostly pink, with black at the base and just inside the outer margin. The underside wings are paler overall. The upper thorax and head of the body are brownish with white stripes, while the abdomen has black-and-white spotting along the top and sides. The antennae are long with compact feathering. The caterpillar eats a variety of plants, including apple, elm, evening primrose, and tomato. Adults feed on flower nectar, using their very long proboscises to probe deep into flowers. The caterpillar is plump, smooth, and blackish; it shows variable amounts of yellow or green stripes and spots, and has a prominent, yellow-orange tail horn.

Hummingbird Clearwing, *Hemaris thysbe*
Family Sphingidae (Sphinx and Hawk Moths)
Size: Wingspan 1.5–2.5"
Range: Throughout Florida
Habitat: Gardens, meadows, roadsides

The hummingbird clearwing is a common, medium-size hawk moth that is active during the day and resembles a small hummingbird, with its rapid, hovering flight and compact body shape. The forewings are narrow and pointed, are reddish brown with olive green at the base, and have large, clear, scaleless patches along their central sections. The hind wings are much smaller and rounded, with similar clear patches. The body is robust, olive green above on the thorax and head and whitish below. The abdomen is dark reddish brown to blackish and terminates in a broad tail tuft. The antennae are long, thick, and black. The caterpillar eats a variety of plants, including hawthorn, honeysuckle, cherry, plum, and snowberry. The adult feeds on flower nectar, using a long proboscis to probe deep into flowers. The caterpillar is fat and bright green, with pale longitudinal stripes and a single yellow to bluish tail horn.

Black Witch, *Ascalapha odorata*
Family Erebidae (Tiger Moths and Allies)
Size: Wingspan 4–6"
Range: Throughout Florida
Habitat: Open fields, urban areas

The black witch is a very large nocturnal moth whose long, pointed forewings, strong flight, and dark shape give the impression of a small bat. There is much folklore concerning doom and foreboding to those who are visited by this moth. The wings are a rich brown overall, intricately scalloped, and mottled with shades of tan and violet. The forewing bears a distinct, kidney-shaped, iridescent blue spot ringed with black and red near the center of the discal cell. The hind wing is squared off, wavy at its lower margin, and bears large, double eyespots. In females, a pale pinkish band runs across the center of both wings. The body is heavily furred, colored various shades of brown, and the moth has long, thin antennae. The caterpillar eats the leaves of a variety of plants from the pea family (Fabaceae), including acacia, cassia, mesquite, and locust. The adult feeds on flower nectar and rotting fruit. The caterpillar is dark brown and smooth, with three pale blotches across the back.

Eastern Tent Caterpillar Moth, *Malacosoma americanum*
Family Lasiocampidae (Tent Caterpillar Moths)
Size: Wingspan 1–1.75"
Range: Throughout Florida
Habitat: Deciduous woodlands, orchards, gardens

The eastern tent caterpillar moth is common, nocturnal, and small- to medium-size. It has a wide body and stubby wings. The forewings are pale gray-brown to rich reddish or chocolate brown, with two white stripes across the interior that sometimes enclose a paler band. The outer wing margins are white and checkered with brown spots; the hind wing is uniformly brown. The body is robust and furry, especially on the thorax, and shows light to dark brown coloration, with a slight dark band on the abdomen. The antennae are brown, broad, and feathered. The caterpillar eats the leaves of plants and trees in the rose family (Rosaceae), including apple, cherry, crabapple, and plum. Adults do not feed. The caterpillar gets its name because it spins silken threads to construct a protective tentlike structure in the forks of branches. It is grayish, marked with blue and red, has a white dorsal stripe, and is covered in fine, long hairs. Periodic infestations of this caterpillar can cause much harm to orchard crops.

SEASHORE
INVERTEBRATES

Atlantic Horseshoe Crab, *Limulus polyphemus*
Family Limulidae (Horseshoe Crabs)
Size: Up to 18"
Range: Coastal Florida
Habitat: Coastal waters with sandy or muddy bottoms

Known as living fossils, today's horseshoe crabs (not actually a type of crab but more closely related to spiders) resemble those that lived 400 million years ago. The Atlantic horseshoe crab has five pairs of flattened legs and two pincers hidden beneath a tough, rounded, horseshoe-shaped shell (carapace) that contains a set of compound eyes. The abdomen has spiked margins, and terminates in a long, sharp-tipped tail. Its color is tan to greenish brown. The horseshoe crab uses the blunt front end of its shell to burrow into sand or mud to hide or limit desiccation during low tides. It swims or walks along the bottom, feeding on crustaceans, mollusks, and marine worms.

Sand Fiddler Crab, *Uca pugilator*
Family Ocypodidae (Fiddler Crabs)
Size: Carapace to 1.5" wide
Range: Coastal Florida
Habitat: Mudflats; quiet, sandy shorelines

The sand fiddler crab is a small inhabitant of beaches and mud-flats. Its most curious aspect is the gross enlargement of one pincer in males (females have two normal-size pincers). The shell (carapace) is trapezoidal, broader in the front; the crab has four sets of legs, two pincers, and its eyes are set on extended stalks. The color varies from shades of brown to nearly white, with darker, purplish marks on top of the carapace. Sand fiddler crabs scoot across the ground on the tips of their legs, feeding during the day on detritus and plant material, and digging into burrows during the night.

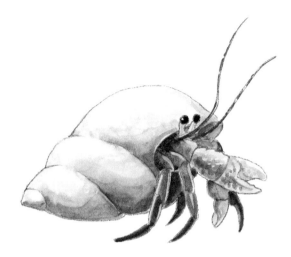

Hermit Crab (many species)
Superfamily Paguroidae (Hermit Crabs)
Size: 0.5–4"
Range: Coastal Florida
Habitat: Shorelines, tide pools, coastal waters with rocky or sandy bottoms

Hermit crabs are not only abundant along the coast, but in pet stores and home aquariums as well. Many species occur in Florida that share certain common characteristics. They have hard carapaces, but the tails are soft, curled, and tapering. For protection, an empty seashell of an appropriate size is chosen, into which the crab inserts its tail. As the crab grows, it discards the shell in favor of a larger one. Hermit crabs have three sets of walking legs, two pincers, and retractable, stalked eyes. Nocturnal and quite social, hermit crabs gather in groups, may live on land or in the water, and scavenge for any available food and algae.

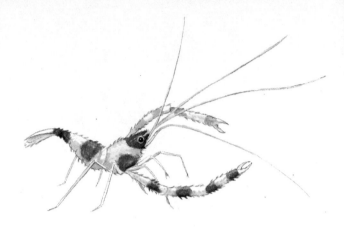

Banded Coral Shrimp, *Stenopus hispidus*
Family Stenopodidae (Coral Shrimp)
Size: Up to 2.5"
Range: Coastal Florida
Habitat: Shallow intertidal zones, coral reefs

The banded coral shrimp is one of many species known as "cleaner shrimp" because of their peculiar feeding behavior. They wave their long, clawed arms to attract passing fish, which come to the shrimp and allow it to pick parasites off the fish's body and eat them. The banded coral shrimp has a small, thin body, with thin legs, broad, long pincers, and long, thin antennae. It is translucent white with bands of orange, red, or purple. The entire body is rough and covered with short spines.

Inshore Longfin Squid, *Loligo pealeii*
Family Lologinidae (Pencil Squids)
Size: Up to 18" (not including tentacles)
Range: Coastal Florida
Habitat: Open to near-shore shallow ocean waters

The inshore longfin squid is abundant and modest-size. It is commercially valuable and important prey for fish, birds, and whales. Its body is smooth and shaped like a narrow, tapered cone; the squid has triangular fins at the front, large eyes, and eight sets of dangling, suction-cup bearing arms as well as two longer tentacles. Its color can change with environmental conditions and the mood of the squid, from translucent pale pink to deep red. All squid propel themselves by forcibly pumping water through a small, funnel-like opening below the eyes. Squid feed on a variety of marine animals, including worms, crustaceans, shrimp, and small fish.

Cushion Sea Star, *Oreaster reticulatus*
Family Oreasteridae (Sea Stars)
Size: Up to 20" in diameter
Range: Coastal Florida
Habitat: Shallow to mid-depth coastal waters with sandy or rubble-strewn bottoms

The cushion sea star is the largest sea star found in Florida. Its body is symmetrical, with a broad, thick center and five (occasionally four or six) stout legs, forming the familiar star shape. The skin is hard and rough above, and fleshy below. Its color is some shade of brown, orange, or red (greenish in juveniles) overlaid with a contrasting, weblike design among the raised bumps. A cushion sea star moves slowly along coastal bottoms using the suction and release of a multitude of tiny "tube feet" on its underside. It covers its prey, such as algae, detritus, crustaceans, and sponges, which it slowly ingests with its central mouth and extendable stomach. Sea stars often move to deeper water in the winter, and younger sea stars may hide in sea grass beds.

Five-holed Keyhole Urchin, *Mellita quinquiesperforata*
Family Mellitidae (Sand Dollars)
Size: Up to 4" in diameter
Range: Coastal Florida
Habitat: Shallow, sandy coastal waters

Also known as the keyhole sand dollar, the five-holed keyhole urchin is one of many species of flattened, disklike urchins. They are most commonly seen after death, washed up on beaches. Their cleaned and bleached shells reveal their familiar, five-rayed flowerlike pattern and keyhole-shaped slots. In life, however, they are adorned with an array of tiny tube feet below, and a velvety carpet of short spines above, colored a shade of brown, green, or purplish gray. Five-holed keyhole urchins burrow into the sand or sit at an angle with one end exposed, catching and consuming small bits of organic matter that drift by or settle in the sand.

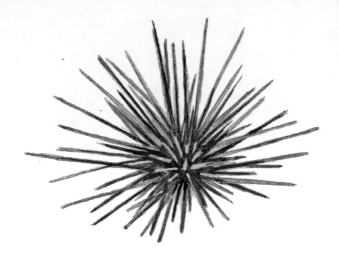

Long-spined Sea Urchin, *Diadema antillarum*
Family Diadematidae (Long-spined Sea Urchins)
Size: 3" diameter (without spines)
Range: Coastal Florida
Habitat: Shallow coastal tide pools, coral reefs

The long-spined urchin is a widespread, prickly sea urchin with long, thin, barbed spines (up to 4") that are hollow and break easily. The body is round and much smaller than the overall bulk of the spines. Adults are colored blackish to dark red-purple, while younger urchins are banded black-and-white. Use caution in tide pools, as the sharp spines can cause painful punctures in the skin. Long-spined urchins form groups at night to feed on detritus, algae, and bryozoans. The urchin leads the material to its mouth at the center of its underside and chews it with strong jaws and teeth.

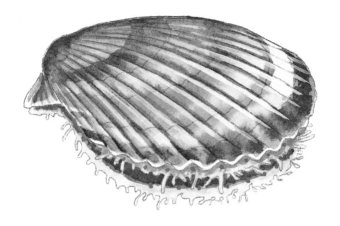

Atlantic Bay Scallop, *Argopecten irradians*
Family Pectinidae (Scallops)
Size: Up to 3" in diameter
Range: Coastal Florida
Habitat: Shallow, sandy coastal waters; areas with sea grass

The Atlantic bay scallop is also known as the blue-eyed scallop, and is important in commercial fisheries. The shell is circular and concave, with 18–20 rounded ridges, a distinctly scalloped margin, and two projecting hind "ears." The scallop can be variously patterned in shades of brown, orange, gray, or greenish gray, sometimes uniform and sometimes with concentric bands. Along the outside edge of the fleshy internal parts is a row of tentacles and numerous blue eyes that detect light and movement. Atlantic bay scallops lie atop the sandy coastal bottoms without burrowing and feed on plankton. They move by rapidly shutting their shells, creating a rush of water that propels them backward.

Index

About the Author/Illustrator

Todd Telander is a naturalist/illustrator/ artist living in Walla Walla, Washington. He has studied and illustrated wildlife since 1989, while living in California, Colorado, New Mexico, and Washington. He graduated from the University of California, Santa Cruz, with degrees in biology, environmental studies, and scientific illustration, and has since illustrated numerous books and other publications, including books in  FalconGuides' Scats and Tracks series. His wife, Kirsten Telander, is a writer, and they have two sons, Miles and Oliver. His work can be viewed online at toddtelander.com.